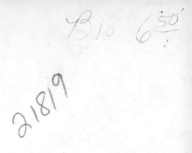

Aram Saroyan

TRIO

Oona Chaplin

Carol Matthau

Gloria Vanderbilt

PORTRAIT OF AN INTIMATE FRIENDSHIP

LINDEN PRESS / SIMON & SCHUSTER

New York   1985

Published by Linden Press/Simon & Schuster
A Division of Simon & Schuster, Inc.
Simon & Schuster Building
Rockefeller Center
1230 Avenue of the Americas
New York, New York 10020
LINDEN PRESS/SIMON & SCHUSTER and colophon are trademarks of
Simon & Schuster, Inc.
Designed by Karolina Harris
Manufactured in the United States of America
1   3   5   7   9   10   8   6   4   2
Library of Congress Cataloging in Publication Data
Saroyan, Aram.
Trio : Oona Chaplin, Gloria Vanderbilt, Carol Matthau.

1. Women—United States—Biography.   2. Chaplin, Oona.
3. Vanderbilt, Gloria.   4. Matthau, Carol.
I. Title.
CT3260.S27   1985   700'.92'2   [B]   85—10196
ISBN 0-671-50919-5

Grateful acknowledgment is made for permission to quote the following copyrighted material:
Epigraph by Leila Hadley from "Gloria" by Patricia Bosworth, published in Town & Country *magazine, January 1978. Reprinted with the permission of* Town & Country.
Epigraph by Ted Berrigan from "Personal Poem #9," published in So Going Around Cities, *Blue Wind Press, Berkeley 1980. Reprinted by permission of the estate of Ted Berrigan, Alice Notley, executor.*
Epigraph by Willa Cather from Lucy Gayheart, *© 1935 by Willa Cather, copyright renewed 1962 by Edith Lewis and the City Bank Farmer's Trust Co. Originally published by Alfred A. Knopf, New York, 1935.*
Epigraph by Lorine Neidecker, untitled poem © 1984 by Cid Corman, literary executor of the Lorine Neidecker estate. Reprinted by permission of Cid Corman.
Epigraph by Truman Capote from "La Côte Basque, 1965," published in Esquire *Magazine, November 1975. © 1975 by Truman Capote. Reprinted by permission of the estate of Truman Capote.*

For Gailyn

ACKNOWLEDGMENTS

I'd like to say a word of thanks to my family and friends, who gave me so much support during this project. I'd also like to thank the following people, who helped in specific ways to bring this book about: Andrew Wylie, Bernard Petrie, Joni Evans, Lee Stevens, Owen Laster, Erica Spellman, Linda Gaede, Anne Bardenhagen, Leslie Ellen, and my editor, Marjorie Williams. My greatest debt, of course, is to the trio of ladies themselves, who told me the stories upon which this book is based. The contribution of my mother, Carol Matthau, has been so extensive it would be more accurate to credit her as my collaborator. At the same time, responsibility for any and all errors and imperfections here is mine and mine alone.

A. S.

CONTENTS

PRELUDE

They were the most radiantly beautiful girls you ever saw. They all had pearly luminous skin, which they powdered pale white, and they had lively eyes and laughed constantly.

—Leila Hadley

Almost Christmas
.
1941

1

THE STREET LIGHTS WENT ON AS SHE AND HER MOTHER were walking through Washington Square Park. It had begun to snow, lightly, not yet sticking. A Salvation Army band at the MacDougal Street corner was playing "Rock of Ages" and the snow seemed, under the street lamp, to be somehow turning around and falling back upward, perhaps in response to the music. It was the usual ruddy band—intent, but not inspired. Poor alcoholic men, uniformed and on the wagon for the moment, their minds freshly starched and, as it were, folded with hospital corners.

Oona's mother pulled her old-fashioned fox coat up closer at her throat and paused on the uptown side of the street. She was off to some cocktail-hour rendezvous, a bookish, old-world rendezvous most likely, where the man in question would remember something of the old days. The Province-town Players, the old "Hell Hole" bar, at which Mr. Eugene O'Neill had held court—no doubt silently. A cult of silence, was it? Oona herself could barely remember exchanging two words with her father.

"All right, my dear," her mother told her, her breath smoky in the street-lit air, "I shan't be very late."

"Well, I think I may be going up to Carol's, Mummy."

"Well, all right dear, but if you go, be sure to leave me a note so I won't worry."

11

"Of course."

She hugged her mother goodbye. A wet finger at her neck suddenly. Snow had melted on her mother's hand. In her forties, she was a tight hugger now, an urgency in her of muscle and sinew—as opposed to anything that might be spoken. Her life, a grip: taut, even bordering on a kind of unconscious violence. She knew her mother wanted to give her something, but it wasn't clear what.

"Goodbye, Mummy."

"Goodbye, dear."

They both turned toward their destinations and then, three or four steps farther on, Oona turned back to look at her mother. But there was a big yellow double-decker sightseeing bus turning at the corner and she wasn't to be seen. It was almost Christmas and, of course, there were still lots of people around who wanted to take a look at Greenwich Village.

By the time Oona got into the apartment it was pitch dark outside, and the snowfall seemed denser. Seeing the random window lights outside—like a strange sort of Morse code across the dark—gave her a quick, sinking sensation, as if she'd forgotten something important in a report she'd just handed in at Brearley, and now it was too late. But she'd graduated high in her class last summer, and when she turned on the lights in the living room everything steadied. She went over to the window to draw the curtains, glancing briefly at the old three-paneled silver picture frame her mother had recently set out again: her family at the beach in Bermuda. In the middle panel, a shot of Daddy and Mummy, Daddy's smile so seemingly difficult for him (a tragedian's smile?), Mummy looking elegant, really exquisite (well, she really *was* a beauty then). In the right-hand panel, Shane, maybe six or seven, looking as though he was trying to remember where he'd put his sand bucket or something. And to the left, barely two, the pouting little sea urchin that she herself had been. Quite the O'Neill, as Mummy would say.

Her father had left Bermuda one day when she was two. He was going to New York to attend rehearsals of *Strange Interlude*. She never saw him again, except for a couple of taciturn visits in very recent years. And by now, of course, whatever early memories she might have reclaimed of him were hopelessly confused with the newspaper and magazine pieces she'd seen about him.

The phone rang and she picked it up off the little walnut table that also held the three-way frame, along with a pile of old *Collier's* her mother had recently retrieved from somewhere.

"Hello."

"You won't believe this!" Thank God. It was Carol. Oona sat down in the wicker chair at the window, still in her black wool overcoat.

"Oh, hi. Are you home?"

"Yes. You're coming up here, right? You won't believe this."

"It's awfully late. Should I? I don't know. What won't I believe?"

"She's going to marry Pat di Cicco. You know the one Cholly Knickerbocker keeps writing about—that she's been dating? He's this very glamorous—I mean really *handsome*—agent . . . in Hollywood."

"She didn't even mention him at the Plaza when we all had lunch together. Of course, you're the only one she really tells things to."

"Listen, it's only five. Come up."

She smiled to herself in her mother's somber little living room, where everything seemed to have suddenly heated up a few very vital degrees.

"Well," she told Carol, luxuriating in the moment, in her friend's life-restoring invitation, "I could take the Fifth Avenue bus and be up there by, oh, say midnight?" She giggled. "Just kidding. It only takes about an hour. When did Gloria tell you all this? I thought she was in California."

"She didn't tell me. I found out in Princeton. You just won't believe it. Listen, get up here or my mother's going to have a long talk with me about my future—when she was seventeen, she was already pregnant (with you know who)—and I can't handle it."

"Oh, God—mothers."

"Darling, are you all right?"

"Yes, yes. Oh, I'm sorry, I don't know, I just went shopping with my mother, only, of course, we didn't buy anything. And I hated all these musty little second-hand shops. I mean she's really this bohemian. She and my father sort of *invented* the whole movement or something. Oh, it's so depressing—"

Carol interrupted her in a sudden conspiratorial whisper. "Oona, I've got chocolates."

"Chocolates?"

"Yes. Loads of them. My mother thinks she's hiding them but I know where they are, and I'm stealing them, box by box. That's too bad about Agnes. Has she got a beau?"

"Well, you know, occasionally there's some man she sort of likes, but all they do is sit around talking about people like Susan Glaspell and George Cram Cook."

"Who are *they?*"

"*I* don't know."

"Well, at least she's got some dignity or something. My mother's a goddamn millinery model who struck it rich; and—take my word for it, darling—all her class is in her hats."

Oona laughed. "Poor Rosheen."

"Sweetheart," Carol answered in her broader, heartier tone, "she's a lot of things, many of them quite awful, but one thing she's *not*—is poor."

Oona laughed again. "Maybe I'll come up now."

"Have you eaten?" Carol asked.

"No, but I'm not hungry." She had found three Indian-head pennies on the table on top of the copies of *Collier's.* Now they were stacked precisely, one on top of the other.

"You will be. I'll have Charlotte put something together for us."

"Oh, that's okay. I mean really. I'm not hungry."

"Sure. Oona's not hungry. I'll see you in an hour. I'll have Charlotte put the roast in now."

"Please!" Oona laughed.

Carol giggled. "Just get up here. I feel a lecture building in my mother. If she knows I'm alone tonight, I'm finished."

2

SHE CAUGHT THE FIFTH AVENUE BUS BESIDE THE WASH-ington Square Arch, and for a while she was absorbed in a well-read library copy of Willa Cather's *Youth and the Bright Medusa*. Then she looked up and discovered they were crossing Thirty-fourth Street, the traffic leaving intricate tire traceries in the snow. It was sticking now, though still nothing heavy. She sighed, relaxing out of the clutch she'd held herself in during the afternoon with her mother. Everything was back again, as it was before she'd somehow misplaced it all in the hazes of her mother's frail destiny. She looked at the black hair where it met the white neck of the young man sitting in front of her. She gazed out from her window seat at passersby in the street. All the different stories on the sidewalk, everyone going somewhere with an idea or two, and, of course, a certain amount of money in their pockets.

Here she was, heading uptown, cozy and anonymous on the Fifth Avenue bus, the famous Oona O'Neill, whom the Stork Club was getting ready to name Debutante of the Year. Jerry Salinger, this young writer she knew, would, of course, give her a big song and dance about how tacky and insincere the Stork Club was being. They were only trying to be chic and boost attendance at her expense, etc. The episode—specifically, the fact that she would even consider accepting such a phony "honor"—would only confirm his worst fears of her superficiality. She would receive these long, sincere, implicitly accusing looks from him. She wasn't ready to cherish his sacred love. Well, she knew what he was really interested in— and it was pretty much the same thing every other boy and man she knew was interested in. That being the case, she might as well marry someone very rich, and very famous— yes, if possible, why not *both?*—who might also have some basic technique down in the area of interest, so to speak.

She could see Jerry getting very upset by such thoughts. His idea was she was supposed to be madly in love with the fact that he was a writer. It was sort of mean to remind him that her daddy was a writer too, hadn't he heard? And, after all, most writers made terrible husbands as well as terrible fathers, according to her own most intimately detailed information.

Well, of course, everybody else would tell her the Stork Club was naming her because she was so popular and beautiful. But Carol was at least as popular, at least as beautiful, also seventeen, plus she was rich, and they weren't naming *her*. And that meant only one thing: Eugene O'Neill.

But—well, fine. Because if she hadn't really had a father, he *had* left her with a name, and that seemed to be some kind of currency or something—and she damned well better use it.

The bus passed a perfect little family now—Daddy, Mommy, and a little bundle in Mommy's arms—standing in front of Rockefeller Center, observing the now fully lit and decorated giant—Norwegian spruce, was it?

On the other hand, look at Gloria—*her* father dead when she was a year old, then that awful custody thing she never talked about, and being raised by her aunt. . . . Then again, maybe Carol's family history was the most insane of all, although she looked and behaved like the first and maybe only seventeen-year-old American fairy princess in history—certainly the first with a big, hearty appetite for hamburgers and chocolates.

Carol's mother, Rosheen, didn't even *tell* her husband, after he married her and moved her and little Carol—whom they got out of the foster home where Rosheen had been forced to put her—into a huge, beautiful apartment on Park Avenue with about eighteen servants, about her *other* daughter, Carol's half-sister, Elinor, who was two years younger than Carol and also in a foster home. She was apparently afraid he'd get mad. When she finally told him, two years after they'd all been living together, he brought Elinor, too, out of the foster home to Park Avenue, and gave her his name, too. It was high tragedy or low comedy, but of course Carol wasn't really about to cry about it—not at this point.

She was having too much fun with the servants and the shopping and making all the boys' eyes pop out and their hearts stop, going gaga at the incredible beauty of her at the dances. The orphan queen, blond with such white skin, white on white, and a mommy who looked young enough to be her sister. Oona sighed and looked out the bus window again.

3

SHE GOT OFF THE BUS AT FIFTY-FIFTH STREET AND WALKED toward Park Avenue. There was now at least an inch of snow, to which the streetlights gave a sort of blond pallor. John, the old doorman with a slight limp, gave her a smile and a nod as he held the door for her.

"Good evening, Miss O'Neill."

"Good evening, John."

The young elevator man with freckles and red hair (what

do they *think* about all day, she and Carol once asked each other) let her off at the fourth floor. She was let into the apartment by James, a slight, white-haired but rather spry old butler. She passed through the mirrored foyer and down the hall to Carol's door, all visibly another scale of human possibility. Like Alice down the rabbit hole. You could do that in New York.

The minute she arrived Carol told her to go into the bathroom and have a bath, to relax; and then, when she was out of the tub, gave her a beautiful nightie to wear and a blue silk robe. Now Carol was sitting on her bed, cross-legged in her nightgown and pink robe, talking to her, while she lay on the other twin bed. This was heaven.

"He's a little boyfriend of my sister's," Carol said with her mouth full. "Are you sure you don't want another of these chocolates with the cherries in it, darling?"

"No, thanks," Oona answered, not looking over, her eyes luxuriating in the crystal labyrinth of Carol's chandelier. Little movies almost coming to life, all the intersecting panes of white light. "Truman?" she said, without breaking out of her reverie. "That's an odd name."

"Truman Capote. Isn't it? But, sweetie, that's the least of it. You know sister. Anyway, right after we talked I took a bath and came out here to put on something fresh—naked, right—and I hear a noise and look up. And see the transom over the door there? Look, darling, right there, so you'll know."

"Oh, yes," Oona said, breaking away only with difficulty from the chandelier and looking over at the glass panel at the top of the door to Carol's room.

"And there's this *face*, looking at me!"

"Oh, my God!" Oona almost sat up, to let Carol know she was responding properly to the drama. But at the last minute, she decided to let it go. It was too hard to unrelax again.

"That's what I thought," Carol went on. "And I screamed

and ran for my robe. And, you know, then he fell off the ladder, I guess. I opened the door after I had something on and yelled at sister. But suddenly then, he steps up, like this little sort of very blond Buster Brown, but with the tiniest little voice, you know, like something out of a fairy tale."

"This is Elinor's *beau?*"

"I don't *know.* Wait'll you hear this. And he says, 'May I speak to you in private?'

"So, I figure, I'm dressed, right? And I knew if he got funny I could beat him up with one hand tied behind my back. So I let him come in here. And he walks around, goes into my bathroom, comes back out and sits down, just looking around at everything, I guess. Now—listen to this—he says to me, in this tiny little voice, 'Oh, honey, don't you *ever* worry about anybody ever seeing *you* naked.'"

"Is he Southern or what?"

"Sort of, I guess. That kind of drawl, you know, but so high and little and he's excited. He says, 'No, you don't ever need to cover up. You're beautiful! I never saw such white skin in my life. Sweetie, you must have been made on the moon!'"

"Jesus!"

"Do you believe it? That's what I thought. And then we sort of talked and he told me how crazy he is about sister. He was quite sweet, you know. But when I saw that face in the transom, I got really terrified."

"What was he doing, anyway?"

"Well, that's the logical question, isn't it? But I got so sort of amazed by his manner and everything, I sort of forgot to ask him. But listen, darling, are you ready to hear about Gloria or do you want to have something to eat first?"

"Like what?"

"Anything. Charlotte can make you a sandwich. Let's go into the kitchen."

19

4

SHE DECIDED TO HAVE A TURKEY SANDWICH ON WHITE bread with lettuce and mayonnaise, and Carol decided she'd have one, too. Charlotte, a large, sweet-natured German lady with a pronounced accent, who seemed to be on night duty in the buzzing, spic-and-span, white-tiled kitchen—it was past nine when they came in—told them she'd bring their sandwiches and Coca-Colas to Carol's room. They returned to their beds, then, both of them taking upright positions in anticipation of the food trays. Oona thumbed through a several-weeks-old copy of *Life* magazine Carol had with a spread on German-occupied France, while Carol started to tell her about Gloria.

"Well, you know how the Princeton thing hap—"

"Carol!" She recognized Rosheen's yell an instant before the door was flung open.

"Don't you dare pull any of that *crap* with me, young lady. When I tell you I want to see you, I mean I want to see you *now.* . . ." Rosheen was standing in a black silk robe in Carol's doorway, as rapturously beautiful as her daughter, even in anger. Suddenly, in the midst of her tirade, she had noticed Oona on the bed opposite Carol's.

"Oh, hello, dear," she said, instantaneously breaking stride into a quietly contained voice, abruptly but unmistakably injected with an English accent. "How are you?"

"Fine, thank you, Mrs. Marcus."

"And how is your mother?" She pronounced it, regally, "muthah."

"Oh, fine," Oona answered, smiling.

"Well, *good* . . . Carol," she said, turning back to her daughter, "we will continue this discussion at another time."

"Yes, mother," Carol answered demurely.

"Goodnight, girls," Rosheen said, closing the door.

"Goodnight," they echoed, and, when the door was closed, took five or six seconds, in acute muscular contortions, holding hands to their mouths, before they allowed a squeak of laughter to escape, knowing they were both on the verge of cascading hysteria and wanting Rosheen to be out of earshot before they erupted. For the next two or three minutes they were unable to look into each other's eyes without collapsing into laughter. Finally, they could look and not immediately laugh.

"Don't you love my mother," Carol said then, "yelling like a goddamn stevedore, and then noticing you and instantly becoming an English lady—*and believing she's got you fooled?*"

Oona fell back onto the bed again for another minute or so, gasping. Carol, inspired by this response, went on.

"Am I wrong or do you have to be very dumb to believe anyone *else* could be so dumb?"

"*Please!*" Oona cried, from her prone, stomach-down position, facing away from Carol.

After a couple of false starts, Carol resumed her story about Gloria.

"Well, you know how the Princeton thing happened, right?"

"Well, Gloria . . ." She had heard about it from Carol, but at the moment Oona could barely remember her own name. Whatever the story was, though, she supposed Gloria's life was a kind of legend to them both. God knows they savored each piece of news of her doings as if it were a sort of riddle they were charged with unlocking.

"Oh, well," Carol continued, "Geoff Jones is Gloria's beau— or was—for a couple of years now. He's the boy who introduced me to her. He's a very good-looking, very sweet boy, and he's at Princeton. So anyway, Gloria calls me one night— she knows that you and I did summer stock when we were in school, of course, and that we read for parts sometimes—

and she says, 'Do you want to be in a play at Princeton?'

"So I said, 'What play?' And she says, 'Well, they're doing a William Saroyan premiere, a play called *Jim Dandy*, and Geoff just called and said they have a part they could use you in.' Probably he wanted *her* to do it, you know, but she was going to California to live with her mother. So I said, 'Sure,' you know. I mean Saroyan is quite interesting, I think. Don't you?"

"Oh, yes." Oona looked up from a still of Olivier in *Wuthering Heights* in *Life*, probably why Carol had kept the issue.

"I mean he's sort of an original, turning down the Pulitzer Prize and everything. The play is wild. It all takes place in an egg."

Oona closed the copy of *Life*. "An egg?"

"Yes, supposedly it signifies the universe or something."

"Oh." The universe? A three-minute egg? Raw? Hard?

"Anyway, I went up for rehearsals—a week of rehearsals, and they'd gotten me a room at a little boarding house like the one we stayed at during the Brown football weekend, remember? Then the play opened for its week run. Brooks Atkinson came up and reviewed it for the *Times*, you know, because it's a new play by Saroyan—come in!"

There had been a knock on the door and now Charlotte entered and put down two small trays, one in front of Oona and the other in front of Carol. They thanked her and she walked back toward the door.

"Enjoy, okay!" Charlotte told them in her high-pitched German English, in a voice that seemed to hover between a laugh and a sob. Then she closed the door again.

"Isn't she sweet?" Carol said just after her first bite.

"Very," Oona answered, starting her own sandwich, which was delicious.

"Anyway, darling, Princeton had a big football weekend, like the one at Brown, and the boarding house where I was staying had been booked for that weekend, in advance you know, so I had to get out of there for the last two nights of the play's run. And I went to stay at Geoff's."

"Oh."

"Yes—but it's not what you're thinking, because he's very sweet and proper and even though it's really just a studio room right near the McCarter Theater, he put up screens for me, and he was just terribly thoughtful and nice. Anyway, he's madly in love with Gloria, of course."

"Of course. No, I wasn't thinking anything, darling."

Carol took a sip of Coke, another bite of her sandwich, and then another sip of Coke, and continued.

"Well, on Saturday afternoon, after we'd been at the theater for some notes and a few changes, during the period where we're sort of supposed to be resting before dinner and doing the show..."

"Unh-hunh."

"Well, I'm lying on my couch behind the screens and Geoff is doing something and the phone rings. It's still afternoon, but it's beginning to get dark. And I hear Geoff pick it up and start talking. At first he's thrilled: 'Oh, hi, darling!'—and laughing. But he starts getting quieter and more serious, and then I can hardly hear him at all. He just sort of fades out, and—I don't remember when exactly, but at a certain point I'm *sure* he's talking to Gloria."

"Right." Oona suddenly felt like getting up, even though she had a few bites of her sandwich left, and half her Coke. She went to Carol's window and gazed across the courtyard at the lighted windows of other apartments as the flakes of snow fell in a somehow leisurely way. In one window, there was a man sitting in an easy chair, wearing black suspenders over a thin-striped shirt, reading the newspaper. Dagwood Bumstead on Park Avenue.

"Well, I know something's up. And the phone call's ending. And I feel sort of terrible for Geoff—but, you know, I don't *really* know what's going on."

"Of course," Oona said from the window. The light uptown was entirely different. It was clearer up here and people did things more crisply. That man's newspaper made a different noise when he folded it. The acoustics were sharper. People were living in the Present, damn it, instead of the netherworld nostalgia of downtown. Her poor mother trying to recapture the past. Just let it go! she wanted to scream. It's night, tonight! Or the sun is shining—right now!

"Well, anyway," Carol went on, "then he hangs up. And there's this dead silence in the room. I'm behind the screen but I can tell he knows I'm in the room. I mean that he's conscious of another person being there at that moment. And I'm lying there and suddenly I can hear my heart thumping in my ears. I'm sort of wishing I weren't there. And then Geoff says, in a voice that's not at all his usual hearty, sort of hail-fellow-well-met manner, you know, but in just a quiet voice, very low, without leaving where he's sitting, he says, 'Do you know who Pat di Cicco is?'"

"To you—?" Oona turned from the window to Carol.

"Yes, to me, because he's hung up the phone and there's nobody else there. And I say, 'Well, I've heard of him,' and sit up, and get up, and walk around the screen. And there's Geoff sitting beside this big worktable he has with his papers and the script and everything, and he doesn't even look up at me, which he would do, but just says, 'I think she's going to marry that guy.'"

"Wow," Oona said at the window, meeting her friend's eyes again.

5

LATER THAT NIGHT, WHEN BOTH WERE IN THEIR BEDS, Carol said softly, "You know what she's doing?"

There was a long pause before Oona could answer because she was sort of toying around at the edge of something that just might have turned out to be sleep.

"Who?" she said finally, at the same time opening her eyes to the room's darkness. No, she was definitely still awake.

"Gloria," Carol answered. "You know what she's doing?"

"What?"

"She's marrying a *man*, darling. Not a boy, but a man. Do you see what I mean?"

"Oh, yes," she said—because, of course, she did. Jerry Salinger, she supposed, was more a man than a boy at this point, but still, even he was just a struggling young writer who might never make a penny.

"I mean the boys at the dances are very sweet," Carol went on, "and I think, in a certain way, I'm even a little in love with Kingdon Gould. But, you know, I mean they're really *very* young men. I mean even Stevie Hopkins, you know, who calls sometimes from his father's office in the White House and is incredibly sweet and charming and funny. But I mean he's just a couple of years older than I am, you know?"

"Like when you go to a restaurant or something..." She could make out the broad outlines of the chandelier again in the darkness.

"Exactly, Oona. With a man, I mean, say, Daddy—well, you know, the maître d' is right there, and the table is set up and everything. Whereas, with a boy, you know, it's not quite

25

the same *even if it is*. Do you know what I mean?"

"You feel *protected* with a man."

"Exactly! In fact, I think she even *said* that to me."

"About Pat?"

"Well, I wasn't sure who she was talking about—we had a long talk on the phone before she left—but she said she'd met someone older and how different it was, and how wonderful."

"But where do we meet these men?" Suddenly she felt sleep on the horizon again. It all seemed so difficult, finally.

"Darling," Carol answered from her bed in the room that was, just then, the inner sanctum of both their lives, "they're everywhere. But you want one who's rich and powerful, of course."

"Of course." Well, yes, of course. She and Carol would need that—whereas Gloria sort of already had it by herself, so to speak.

"So that narrows it down a little. We should, though. We should do exactly what Gloria's doing."

"Oh, we should," Oona echoed in the dark.

PART ONE

feminine marvelous and tough

                          Ted Berrigan, The Sonnets

Springtime in the Rockies
·
1946

1

H OW IN THE WORLD CAROL HAD TRACKED HER DOWN was a mystery. But then she always seemed to know, instinctively, how to get through. Here was this really gorgeous blond girl, with—you would think—a head full of sweet nothings, who had fallen for Bill Saroyan the way another girl might fall down a flight of stairs, and somehow or other Carol would land on her feet. It really seemed to be some sort of instinct.

So the phone had rung on the wall of the ranch house in Wyoming at eleven that morning: one of those crank phones that you had to wind up, and the ring sounded as though the phone was sort of coming out of a coma. First hardly there at all, then quite loud. Then dying out again. All in the space of one ring. And Tex, the foreman of the ranch, had picked it up. She thought it must have been the local feed store or something like that. But then Tex walked over to the table where she and Leopold were finishing their coffee.

"Mrs. Stokowski," he said, "it's for you."

She and Leopold exchanged a look that involved more of her personal history than Gloria wanted to consider—ever. Then, of course, there was the dread specter of the press, relentlessly hounding her since her breakup with Pat di Cicco. What had happened between them?—they wanted to know. As if she could blithely announce to the world that in marrying Pat she maybe hadn't been doing much more than divorcing her mother and her aunt, and once that was accomplished...

"For me?" Gloria said, looking up out of a writhing chaos of possibilities.

"Yes, ma'am. Sounds like long distance."

"Go ahead, darling," Leopold interjected, smiling warmly at her. "Have a feeling it's good news. Don't be afraid, sweetheart." As always, his accent was unaccountably reassuring.

Gloria got up from the table and walked to the phone in her three-week-old cowboy boots. She picked up the receiver and said hello.

"Darling, it's Carol. I'm so sorry."

"Oh, *sweetheart*," she answered, her heart melting with her dearest friend's first words. "How *are* you? Darling, *where* are you?"

"Oh, I'm just in dumb old San Francisco. *You're* where the excitement is. I just wish I could get Bill to give up writing and become a cowboy. I just have a feeling he'd be good with horses...."

Gloria was laughing the way she usually did after a moment or two in that zany mental altitude that was Carol's alone. Yet at the same time, she knew something was up. She caught her breath, stopped giggling, and tried to fill her in.

"Darling, Leopold and I have just had breakfast on this dude ranch and we're all about to go out and see the *branding*. ... Oh, Carol, it's very exciting, and terribly sad. I miss you."

"Gloria, you've got to come here. I'm leaving Bill. You've got to come and help me pack. You know I wouldn't ask unless it were *absolutely* a matter of life and death."

"Oh, sweetheart. Of course."

"I've got to get out of here. He treats me like dirt. *Dirt*. Gloria, swear to me you'll never repeat this to a soul. I'd die. I swear it."

"Oh, but you don't even have to *say* that, darling. It's *understood*."

Leopold was understandably bewildered. The sixty-three-year-old shaggy-maned maestro, world renowned for his majestic, richly textured renderings of Brahms and Tchaikovsky, was in the midst of a difficult period professionally; his NBC broadcasting contract had been canceled a year before. Just now, after a whirlwind courtship in New York, Florida, California, and Mexico, he and Gloria, the beautiful twenty-one-year-old Vanderbilt heiress, only recently divorced from Pat di Cicco, were on their honeymoon. Concurrently, he was taking a breather before conducting the 1946 summer season at the Hollywood Bowl.

Gloria herself, however, knew a sort of instantaneous relief at the prospect of seeing Carol, and of getting away from... ranch life. She was sure she had seen enough herds of cattle to have absorbed whatever lesson might have been in it for her. And the branding had a brutal... majesty almost, she supposed. But *really.* Enough was enough. Leopold was working something out, though. She could see that. Possibly something acoustical. What the West *sounds* like, maybe. He would bring the cattle lowing and the thunder of the herds into the summer season he'd be conducting at the Hollywood Bowl. He would make the *Grand Canyon Suite* come alive with the orchestral echoes and equivalents of noises he had heard in the real West.

"But, darling, this is something Carol and Bill work out among themselves, no?"

"No, darling. She said it was *over.* Finished. They're getting a *divorce.* I've got to help her. I've got to go there and help get her and the baby out of there and take them down to the house on Beverly Crest, and let them... recover."

The maestro looked from his enchanting young wife to Tex, the big, solemn foreman of the ranch.

"Tex, now, tell us how we do this. How do we—" He turned back to his wife. "Dearest, I won't come. You and Carol must do this alone. Is that so?"

"Oh, yes. No, you mustn't come. Because you must go on with *your work.*"

"Tex, how do we get my dear one to San Francisco?"

"Mr. Stokowski, we'd have to have a mule-pack to get up through the ridge. And then to get down to the Union Pacific depot in Sherbot. There's no way the jeep'll go through up there."

So she had had two suitcases packed onto the mule, and now she rode on a pony that Pete, one of the ranch hands, small and dark, with a red bandanna, led on foot by the reins. It was warm, and quiet. Somewhere in the Rockies. This *was* the Rockies, wasn't it? Springtime in the Rockies. The color was marvelous—clay reds, just like the color photographs in her old encyclopedia at Mrs. Whitney's. And every so often some kind of violet showed its head in the middle of the hardness as they clomped along in the sunlight.

And as she rode, Gloria would think of Carol, remembering.

For a long time before she met her, Gloria kept hearing about Carol from Geoff Jones or Fletcher Godfrey or Jay Eddy. They called her "the Baby." It was the Baby this and the Baby that. And she's so pretty. And so witty. And she goes to Dalton. And her parents have a big apartment on Park Avenue that's open almost all the time.

And so finally Geoff, who was Gloria's first beau, brought Carol out to Mrs. Whitney's in Old Westbury one afternoon with Jay and Fletcher, and Gloria served them all dinner in her room. They played Cugat records and danced. And she really was—well, dazzling.

Here was this fifteen-year-old girl, the same age as Gloria, who was a sort of cross between Jean Harlow and a Christmas tree angel, and she'd say things that would sound absolutely as if you were hearing her make some terrible mistake, but it *wasn't* a mistake because she had decided about it and her mind was very, very clear, and everything would turn out to be perfectly all right after all.

She had once overheard some boy at a dance say to Carol, "You only like famous people." It was one of those moments Gloria had panicked for her friend and instantaneously wondered whether Carol liked *her* because she was famous. But Carol was perfectly in control.

"That's right," Carol replied immediately to the boy. "They're all terrific, and you stink." And then she stuck her tongue out at him, and he laughed; but, after a moment more for the sake of appearances, he moved on, definitely out of his depth.

She really wasn't a person who was going to be topped by just anybody's mean little mind. Her mind was big and strong enough to fend for itself just about anywhere—and yet, as Gloria knew her, she didn't provoke her own female jealousy. She was too darling, and, in her own way, too openly vulnerable for that. She was, she supposed, the only true friend Gloria had ever had in the world.

"Would you like a drink of water, Mrs. Stokowski?" Pete asked her, bringing the pony to a halt beside a boulder.

"Oh—yes. Thank you."

"Sure," Pete said, handing her an unopened canteen, and then taking a swig on his. "It's another hour or so, I reckon. And that'll put you in plenty of time for the two o'clock headed into California."

"The one to Oakland."

"I reckon that's the one."

The water tasted divine, and with the animals still, the mountain silence was something deeper than she could have imagined—you could practically hear the sunlight moving. For a moment, she wished Leopold and everyone were here. He would say something wonderful and they all would marvel at his genius. Although if he said "The sun is shining," she knew—because she had seen it—people would be no less awestruck. They would look back and forth at each other, and their looks would say, "Did you hear what he said? 'The sun is shining.' Isn't that wonderful?"

Well, maybe genius *was* that ability to see the obvious with complete, childlike amazement.

During the first week of their tour of dude ranches, Gloria had been reading a book of poems by Wallace Stevens and she had shown Leopold one about the flight of an eagle—a marvelous poem that might have been written in their very surroundings. The maestro had read it aloud with his passionate declamatory style, his hands flying out the way they did when he conducted. And then, immediately after, he had declared that he must write Wallace Stevens a letter.

She knew better than to ask whether or not they knew one another. As an internationally recognized musical genius, Leopold was a member of an elite: his name alone opened not just doors, but hearts. Gloria was famous, but Leopold was virtually adored. And he was constantly firing off letters to others in this international pantheon: Chaplin, Roosevelt, Churchill. He would never hesitate to share a moment of revelation with one of these kindred spirits.

To Wallace Stevens he wrote that he himself had always felt that life should be like the soaring flight of an eagle, captured so handsomely by the poet in the poem he and Gloria had just read. A week or so later, when their mail was forwarded, they found among the pieces a reply from Stevens. Dear Mr. Stokowski, the poet had written, Thank you for your letter. I agree with you that life should be like the soaring flight of an eagle. Sincerely, Wallace Stevens.

A turkey buzzard was circling in a wide arc above them. Pete took back her canteen.

"All set?"

Gloria nodded, smiled. Pete gave the reins a tug and they were off again.

• • •

Could Bill Saroyan be like Leopold? He was younger, of course, and, at least to Gloria, quite a bit scarier. He was so loud. Carol had told her he was slightly deaf and not to be frightened, but Bill really, most of the time, shouted. He had nothing of Leopold's sweetness and composure, although she supposed he might be just as famous and well loved. Or almost.

A few months before, some people had been trying to get Leopold to conduct the score for a movie about Jesus, and Gloria had suggested—quite sincerely, at least at that moment—that, of course, he should *play* Jesus, too. (It really wasn't, after all, the sort of role you could see going to Errol Flynn or even Tyrone Power.)

Leopold, who up to that moment had been absorbed in a consideration of some detail of the negotiation, paused and looked over in her direction without quite focusing on her.

"Yes," he said after a moment, his eyes still fixed on the middle distance, "—perhaps."

But Bill Saroyan *behaved* as if he had some kind of divine mission to hold the center of attention every moment you were with him. Unlike Leopold, he really never listened to *anyone*, so far as she could see.

Which was why it was so crazy to see Carol with Bill. Really, Bill Saroyan was some kind of demon, some absolute force of nature. He would come into a room and just take over. He was so loud, of course—but he was also very handsome, and some of the stories he told were, Gloria supposed, really quite marvelous and funny.

But he would take over lock, stock, and barrel. And Carol was like another person when she was with him. Here was this dark Armenian and there was Carol, all white, and they made some kind of new chemical compound that didn't seem to effect any very significant change in Bill, but totally transformed Carol.

She must be, Gloria decided as Pete led her pony through a shaded downhill pass and she held her arm up to avoid getting stuck with briars, really afraid of him. She could still be cute, and funny, but she really *deferred* to Bill—well, *she* did to Leopold, too, of course; but Leopold was so devoted, so caring, so loving. And Bill wasn't like that at all. He kept Carol in a state of constant anxiety, wondering all the time if he really loved her. All that aplomb she carried around, the daffy authority she commanded, just seemed to crumble.

She was suddenly like a naked little girl, shivering out in the cold world, wondering if Bill would ever really love her. Gloria had never *seen* anybody so in love in her whole life. Carol had a whole new set of habits, suddenly: getting out her compact every two or three minutes to check herself in the mirror; pushing her perfect nose up as she checked herself because Bill had once mentioned he liked that kind of nose. She just went crazy.

2

THAT NIGHT, INSTALLED IN HER SLEEPER ON THE TRAIN, Gloria kept the blinds up and watched the darkness hurtle by. The train wheels made a sort of lulling, melancholy music. She found something familiar and comforting, too, in all the train-ride amenities: the little soap packages, the ice-water trays, the redcaps smiling and flattening themselves in the aisles to let you pass.

In the depths of her childhood, these compartments—or those on ships—had sometimes seemed as close to a home as anything she knew. When Gloria's father—the dissolute Reginald "Reggie" Vanderbilt—died of acute alcoholism at the age of forty-four while she was still an infant, her mother, a beautiful, fun-loving, and still very young woman, whose head, alas, Gloria had seen, really *was* full of sweet nothings, took up traveling. International traveling. And little Gloria and her nurse, Dodo, lived from day to day out of hotel suites and train and boat compartments, or else were left behind entirely at their "homes" in London, Paris, the English countryside, the South of France. The back of the chauffeur's head became a more familiar landmark than any garden tree or hideout. She became, paradoxically, the orphan of a life conditioned by extreme wealth.

During those years, she would pick up a little wrapped-up package of soap and smell it as if it might impart the wisdom of some very great book. But it only smelled sweet—like her mother. Dodo would read her a story about two children, a brother and a sister, who lived in the country with their mother and their father and a very old grandfather. They had a farm with chickens and cows, and the children shared a room and played secret games about the weather that no one else knew.

Even now, at twenty-one, Gloria could feel at times a sudden, choked yearning for a place like that somewhere: some familiarity of years rather than the gathered coincidences of only moments through the years. It was almost as if space had replaced time in her mother's life: the geography of an international high-life seemed to keep the clock perpetually at the stroke of midnight. And home was wherever the suitcase opened and the evening dress emerged. Little Gloria saw her beautiful mother, Big Gloria, and her twin sister, Thelma, standing before their full-length mirrors in the hotel suites of the continent, and their images multiplied like some magical cancellation of the clock, which seemed to preside over the lives of the brother and the sister in the story she would ask Dodo to read her over and over again.

The problem was, there was so little to hold on to—other than to her mother (mostly off somewhere, anyway), or Dodo. The numberless shaggy-dog stories that, in the end, probably made up the remembered childhoods of most people, at least in the books she'd read, wouldn't be hers. All her childhood narratives would be abruptly truncated—if they even had time to begin at all—in meeting the next scheduled ship, or train, or automobile.

The train seemed to be coming into a station; they were slowing and passing lamps on the platform, little islands of illumination. Gloria lowered the blinds and decided to get ready for bed, hoping that she would sleep at least a little before she arrived to see Carol in the morning. She had telegraphed her from the train station in Sherbot the details of her arrival, by ferry from Oakland into San Francisco, and she hoped that she would see her face when the boat docked.

The choking noise of the brakes was followed by the hissing. Gloria put on her nightgown, got under the covers, and turned off the lights. This time, too, she was on an unknown mission—something as hard to understand, in its way, as all those incomprehensible childhood voyages. Except that her friend would be there at the end of the journey. Carol, whom she really knew and loved, would be there. That was the difference.

Carol caught Gloria's wedding bouquet, which Gloria had thrown to the crowd of well-wishers in Santa Barbara at her first wedding as she emerged from the church on Pat di Cicco's arm and began to descend the steps to the waiting limousine. Carol would be the next to marry, Gloria knew then. But there seemed to be no end to the steps, literally thousands of them, and suddenly she and Pat seemed to be tap-dancing, while the photographers' shutters clicked and the flashbulbs went off. "Come on along, come on along—it's Alexander's Ragtime Band." Gloria found that she could make a certain staccato run of taps that fascinated her: her body obeyed an impulse that created its own kind of music.

She was suddenly dancing—and in front of everybody. There was her mother, and Thelma, at the side, along with the Duke of Windsor.

And, in another part of the crowd, there was Mrs. Whitney playing some instrument with evident zest—was it a French horn? It was exhilarating and at the same time exhausting. Pat seemed to be forever dancing up the stairs, and then down again, and she was eager to go—to get into the car, if it was still even there, and be gone into their own life together.

Finally, she reached the limousine and it seemed to be locked, and inside, suddenly, on the other side of the glass, was Carol's face, looking worried and then making faces of grief. Gloria wondered if Bill was in the car, too, before feeling Pat take her hand again and, when she turned around, lead her up the stairs where she could see the orchestra, and Leopold suddenly there, tapping on the lectern, trying to bring the musicians to order before beginning another number.

Tap, tap, tap . . . Tap, tap, tap . . .

Then Gloria was awake; the tapping was coming from outside her door.

"Who is it?" she called. The door was locked.

"Redcap, ma'am. We'll be arriving in Oakland in forty-five minutes. Breakfast is being served in the dining room." He didn't try to open the door.

"Thank you."

"Yes, ma'am."

She pulled up her nightshade to daylight—the outlying urban sprawl of empty lots, little corner grocery stores, three-story houses. She pulled the shade down again, switching on the lights, until she had dressed. The sun seemed to be going in and out. She washed her face in the tiny, stainless steel bathroom compartment. Before packing, she rang and ordered coffee.

3

AT THE STATION, A REDCAP GOT HER TWO BAGS TO THE ferryboat that docked at the station and would take her to San Francisco. It was overcast. She stood on board the boat during what seemed to be a midday lull in commuter traffic. There was an old man in a yellow rain slicker reading a *Chronicle* (ONE GUARD KILLED, NINE INJURED IN ARMED REVOLT ON ALCATRAZ, read the headline) and a young woman with two little boys, both very bundled up against the wind. It was very windy on board. For a while there were several sea gulls flying around the boat, squawking at themselves, the boat, the sea.

Then they were putting into shore, and an excitement, bordering on panic, filled her heart. What was it Carol had wanted her to come for? To get her and the baby, Aram, out of the house. That was it. She and Bill were separating. They were going to get a divorce.

She was going to have her friend back again from the crazy isolation Bill had enforced on the marriage—not allowing them to talk on the phone, making Carol return the pearls Gloria had given her while Bill was overseas in the army.

"I've had the full pleasure of really having this gift," Carol had told her on the day Bill had forced her to give them back. "And nothing can ever change that or take it away, darling."

How dear she was!

Carol was waiting on the other side of the turnstiles holding the little boy, Aram, in her arms, as Gloria came through with the porter who carried her bags.

"Darling, you look *so* beautiful," Carol whispered as they hugged. "Uh, don't look. I'm a fat cow."

"Sweetheart, you look ravishing. What are you talking about?" Carol, as always, looked radiantly beautiful with that flowerlike freshness that seemed to be hers alone. Any slight plumpness was not at all unbecoming.

"Taxi this way, ma'am," said the porter, and they followed him through the glass-paneled doors to the street. It seemed to be just on the verge of raining. Aram was playing with a strand of Carol's hair he had gotten free from her scarf.

Gloria tipped the porter, who had put her two suitcases into the back trunk of a taxi. Then she followed Carol and the little boy into the car.

"Twenty-seven twenty-seven Taraval Street," Carol told the driver. "That's off Nineteenth Avenue." Then she turned to her friend. "Gloria, my God," she said, in that special breathless way of hers, "you're *so* divinely beautiful."

"Oh, sweetheart, please. *You're* the beauty."

The taxi pulled out and began negotiating the noontime traffic. It was now lightly raining. The driver turned on his windshield wipers.

"No, no. Listen, you know Bill said a great thing to me once. He said that no one could be truly beautiful who didn't have a touch of race in their looks. Do you know what I mean?"

"Well, of course, but really how could you think . . . I mean here I am bearing the name of the great *robber baron*, darling . . . I mean I'm a *Vanderbilt*, for God's sake." She was laughing, and so was Carol now, too. "I mean I'm just *not* a candidate for the ethnic look, now, am I?"

Carol stopped laughing, and studied her friend with great seriousness.

"But of course you are. *Of course* you are. Oh, but Gloria, you *must* know that. . . ." Gloria knew only that she felt as happy, at that moment, as she could be. Carol could do that to her even in the midst of the terrible situation she knew her friend was going through at that moment.

"But I want to hear about *you*. I mean are we going to just pick up some bags at the house and then go right on to a hotel? The Fairmont, darling?"

"Sweetheart," Carol said, giving her a suddenly rather serious look, "that's all changed."

"Changed?" Gloria felt a sudden ripple of fright running along her spine. Bill *was* frightening.

"Yes. I don't know what I could have been thinking. I guess I was just so stunned by how beautiful you really are—no, really. Do you know what you remind me of—and always have? Do you know the *Red* and *Blue Fairy Books*?"

"Yes, but..."

Carol looked at her with a slight half-smile that deepened as she recited:

> Lips as red as blood,
> Eyes as black as night,
> Skin as white as snow,
> Hair as dark as ebony...

"That's you. No, I mean it. That's what you've always been like to me."

"Sweetheart, *thank you*. But you must—you really must tell me what's going on with you and Bill."

Carol looked away for a moment, and Aram, sitting between the two of them, again reached up for his mother's hair.

"You've just got to get free of his *tyranny*, Carol," Gloria added.

"Gloria, you've got to help me get him back," Carol said, turning back to her.

Gloria was startled. "Oh, but you're kidding?"

"No," Carol said, aware that she had upset her friend, and making her voice slower and as clear and sober-sounding as she could manage. "It's funny, between me and Bill. I know what I said on the phone and I'm *so* glad you're here. But, underneath everything—really, darling, this is the deepest truth—I know he loves me, and I know I love him. Anyway, sweetheart, I've got another piece of news—I'm preggers."

"Oh, but you're *not?*"

Gloria felt as though the wind had been knocked out of her, but Carol only nodded with that sort of half smile that seemed to say, "It's funny, isn't it, how life goes?" For a moment, Gloria felt an anger stirring in her at this: the absurd end of her long odyssey. Was it, after all, a false alarm? How *could* she? Yet, somehow, there was something in Carol's expression—radiant and waiflike at the same time—that allowed her to put these thoughts aside, and she struggled to follow her friend in this new direction.

"Well, I mean, whatever you want to do. Of course."

"Gloria, I'm so glad you're here. Really, I am."

"But, Carol, where is he? Is he at home—now?"

"Well, see, that's the thing. He's been up in his office since before I called. He's got his own studio up there with a kitchen and his own entrance and everything—and he won't come down."

"Well, have you tried to—to talk with him?"

"Well, he's got his own phone, and I did call him yesterday—but he wouldn't talk to me. But I know he thinks I'm still mad at him, and if he just knew that I wasn't—anymore— I know everything would be okay again."

"Are you sure?"

"Gloria, you've got to help me. Promise me you will." Carol's voice was suddenly full of real gravity. And if it was her friend's genuine plea, as it seemed to be, why, of course, Gloria would help.

"Oh, I will, of course. You know I will."

"Good!" Carol said suddenly in a completely different, comically curt voice, and giggled.

4

2727 TARAVAL WAS A THREE-STORY ROW HOUSE, AND Carol, holding Aram, followed by Gloria and the taxi driver, holding Gloria's two bags, climbed the stairs up to the front door.

Gloria and Carol had a fight about who would pay the driver, a man in his sixties who spoke with a heavy Italian accent. Gloria won, but Carol gave him an extra dollar for "being so nice." He thanked them both and left, and Carol closed the door.

It was rather dark in the house and Carol turned lamps on in the big front room overlooking Taraval Street. Aram sat down on the dark green carpet and began playing with his cars and trucks. What had happened to all that money Bill had made before the war? The house was quite a comedown from the apartment they'd had on Sutton Place South in New York during the war.

"Darling, sit down and let me get you some coffee," Carol told Gloria. "That's Bill flushing the loo."

Gloria sat down on a sofa upholstered in a cabbage rose chintz with a low coffee table in front of it, glad about the coffee coming, and it was a moment before she let herself hear the second part of what Carol had said. When she did, she was puzzled.

"What did you mean about Bill and the loo just now?"

Carol was now standing in the middle of the front room, as if in a trance. She pointed a finger above her head.

"He's standing right over us," she said to Gloria. "Can you hear him? That noise is the loo upstairs. He just flushed it."

"Oh."

It was strange having Bill over the living room.

"Darling, what's he *doing* up there?"

"Well," Carol answered in an even but animated tone, as though she had just hit on a topic of lively general interest, "this morning he got up and showered and shaved, and made himself some breakfast. And then he wrote a story, probably, or maybe it was a long letter. He writes over there." She pointed to the front corner of the ceiling.

Gloria's nervousness increased.

"Well, darling, what do you suppose he's doing now?"

"Right now?"

"Yes, right above us," Gloria answered, keeping her voice low.

"Oh, he's just standing for a minute, thinking. He does that a lot."

Suddenly the ceiling made creaking noises and Carol followed the noises over to above the corner of the sofa where Gloria sat. Carol kept her eyes on the ceiling for a moment, and then she began to nod from Gloria to the ceiling, and back again.

"Darling, please," Gloria said, unable to contain herself any longer, "what's going on?"

Carol nodded back to her as though everything were now in order.

"See, he's making a telephone call. That's where the phone is—right there," Carol said, pointing to a spot just above her on the ceiling.

"Well, who do you think he's talking to?"

"His mother or his bookie," Carol said with matter-of-fact certainty. And then she seemed to come out of it. "I'm sorry, sweetheart. Let me get you some coffee. Gloria, you've got to think I'm stark, raving mad. I've just been following Bill around the ceiling. And you want to know something? I *am*— I've gone crazy, darling."

"Mama gone crazy!" Aram shouted, pushing a large green dump truck under the coffee table.

45

"No, sweetheart," Carol told the two-year-old boy, "Mama's just joking." Turning to Gloria, she added: "See, that's the kind of thing Bill might hear him say and make a federal case out of. Oh, it's just insane."

5

LATER THAT AFTERNOON, A HOUSEKEEPER, A BENT-OVER old woman with the improbable name of Mercedes, came in to do housecleaning, feed Aram, and, as it turned out, make scrambled eggs and toast and coffee for Carol and Gloria, who sat at the kitchen table overlooking the backyard. They had heard Bill leave his upstairs apartment an hour or so before, just after the sky had cleared up, and go out on an errand somewhere. Now the sun, playing hide-and-seek, would occasionally cast the shadows of the red china sugar bowl and the salt and pepper shakers on the table.

Aram sat in the middle of the kitchen floor, grinding coffee with an old-fashioned coffee grinder. Mercedes had used some of what he ground in the pot she had on the stove.

"Oh, Gloria," Carol said as the food was brought to the table, "sometimes I wonder why I didn't marry one of those little rich boys at all the debutante dances in New York."

Mercedes put down a plate of scrambled eggs and toast for Gloria and one for Carol. Then she brought two cups of coffee.

"Umm, Mercedes," Carol said with a special voice and a twinkle to the old woman, "you're spoiling me. You know how mad Bill would be if he saw you do that."

"Oh, it's no bother, Mrs. Saroyan."

"Thanks, sweetheart," she said in a voice that was suddenly rather hearty. "Anyway, you and I won't tell that big fuck, okay?" And she burst into surprisingly deep laughter, and Gloria laughed too, while the older woman, smiling but not saying anything, turned back to the stove.

Although Gloria was very hungry, she found herself balking at the plate before her. The scrambled eggs appeared to be green. Carol, on the other hand, seemed oblivious to this and lit into hers like there was no tomorrow—but then, she always did. She was the fastest eater Gloria had ever known. Well, maybe Oona Chaplin was a match for her.

"Darling, how's Oona?" she asked Carol now.

"Divinely happy," Carol said. She swallowed, and then continued. "She's found the greatest man in the world, I guess."

"Oh, darling, really," she said, laughing. "That sounds too good to be true."

"Well," Carol went on seriously, "all I know is Oona. And you know, in a funny way, I think she's never really been happy before. But now, with Charlie, she is."

It was so odd to think of Oona, married now for—what, three years?—to Chaplin. She hadn't seen her since the wedding, but Carol had told her all about it. The whole thing was so romantic, turning up for a screen test and having this genius fall instantly in love with you. People had talked, of course— Oona was so young, and Charlie was in his fifties. But Gloria wasn't about to throw any stones in that particular direction. She knew from experience what a comfort an older, seasoned man could be just as a matter of course. No, she was as happy for Oona as she was for herself with Leopold.

"How often do you see her?" Gloria had her fork in the scrambled eggs but still hadn't lifted it.

"Well, we went down to Hollywood for a few days for Bill to do some business and we all had dinner together. They've got this marvelous, big house up on Summit Drive, and Charlie's full of ideas for his new film, *Monsieur Verdoux*. He and Bill get along. Listen, now that you're going to be living there, you've got to phone her."

"Oh, I will once I get that place furnished. I think Leopold knows him."

"Do it before," Carol said, after a sip of coffee. "She'd love to see you. And Charlie doesn't stand on ceremony. You know, of course, she's pregnant again?"

"Really? How old is the first? Geraldine?"

"She's two."

"Mrs. Saroyan," Mercedes interrupted them, "shall I take Aram downstairs now that it's not raining?"

"Yeah," Aram said, looking up from the coffee grinder, "Aram want to play now!"

"All right, darling," Carol said, addressing herself to Aram. "We'll be right here when you get back. Mommy's going to talk to Auntie Gloria."

The old woman and the little boy went out the door and down the outside stairs that led from the kitchen to the backyard.

"Um, Carol, the scrambled eggs are—sort of..."

"Oh, I know, sweetheart," Carol replied, with toast in her mouth and the coffee cup near her lips. "They're green. She *always* does that. I don't know what it is. But if it were anything bad I'd have been dead long ago—because it's *all* she ever cooks."

"Oh, good. I just wasn't sure."

Gloria now tasted her eggs, and, as her caution gradually surrendered to her hunger, proceeded to clean her plate, too. She took a sip of coffee and was startled by how good it was. "Mmm."

"Isn't it good? It's Bill's big thing. He's got it upstairs too. It's his secret. He drinks six or seven cups each morning. He has three or four at breakfast. And then drinks three or four while he works. No wonder he can't relax."

"Is he like that all the time? I mean so sort of *charged?*"

"Well, it's strange. I mean I've never known anyone so driven, you know. But he also spends days in his bed when he gets tired. So it sort of balances out, I guess."

"He sounds really *scary*, darling. Is he—I mean does he get—?"

"Violent, you mean?"

"Well, yes."

"Well, he's pushed me a couple of times—you know, against a wall. But that's it. So far. Keep your fingers crossed for me, okay?"

"Oh, Carol, I'm just so *worried* about you. I mean, are you sure you want to stay here like this?"

"Oh, sure. I mean I don't exactly know *what* I want to do— or what I *should* do about him—but it'll work out. Won't it?"

She looked at Gloria, and smiled; Gloria smiled back.

"Anyway," Carol said, "I started to tell you—well, remember when I came out to L.A. for your wedding with Pat?"

"I dreamed about it last night."

"Really—my God. I thought you'd forgotten his name by now."

They both laughed.

"He didn't deserve you. He didn't. Anyway, you remember I stayed with your mother and Thelma on Maple Drive. God, they were sweet. They were making those Princess and the Pea Christmas presents out of matchboxes, you know, and they'd use a real little pearl for the pea."

"Oh yes."

Suddenly the sun cast very pronounced shadows off everything on the table.

"And every party we went to they'd show me how to dress— and make sure my sash was at the right angle and everything. And, well, you know, of course, there was that night that I met Bill."

"Of course."

"And, well, the fireworks sort of went off in my head and I began walking around like a zombie all day waiting for him to call. And, of course, your mother and Thelma noticed. They'd have had to. I was like a little robot. And Gloria said— did I tell you this?"

"No, I don't think so."

An airplane was going by outside.

"Well, see, she knew I'd been dating Kingdon in New York. And Stevie Hopkins, and, you know, the little gang at the dances. And she said to me, 'Well,' she said, 'William Saroyan. Yes, he's an artist, and I'm sure he's marvelous. But Carol, don't forget that those boys you're dating in New York— those boys come from some of the richest families in America, and they're all going to be very important men.' God, if only I'd listened to her."

"But, sweetheart, I know you don't mean that. Because if you did, you'd come with me right now and leave this place. And *marry* one of them."

"I know that's what I *should* do, but I love Bill—so I can't."

"Well, what do you want to do?"

"Oh! I think that's him. He's coming up the stairs. Maybe he'll come in."

Gloria's heart froze. The idea of seeing this man was suddenly more than she could handle. Suppose he threw a fit when he found her there with his wife? Carol listened. The steps seemed to pause; then they continued and Bill went up to the next landing. Gloria was more relieved than she could tell Carol, and, at the same time, she was surprised at herself for being so frightened.

6

THAT NIGHT SHE SLEPT ON THE SOFA IN THE FRONT ROOM while Carol stayed in Aram's room on the extra bed. Carol had wanted her friend to have the bed, but Gloria was afraid the little boy would wake up in the middle of the night and want his mother. Usually Carol slept upstairs with Bill, and would come down to Aram, if he cried, through a door at the top of the stairway off the living room. Bill now kept this door locked.

Somehow, Gloria couldn't shake her fear of Bill. What if he decided suddenly to come down in the middle of the night and sort of thrashed around in the dark and discovered her on the sofa and thought, in the darkness, that she was Carol? She could see herself struggling, but she'd be half afraid, at the same time, to just say "Bill, it's Gloria!" If he thought she were Carol he might try to make love to her. But if he found out she was Gloria, who knew what he might do? He might just go crazy and . . . there was no sense even thinking about it.

She listened to the occasional cars that passed outside in the dark: another life (or more than one) going by inside each— first barely audible in the distance, then right beneath the window, then fading into oblivion again.

For some reason, she found herself thinking of Mrs. Whitney, at that moment a strangely comforting presence somehow. For all her faults, this lady—her father's sister, a Vanderbilt who had married a Whitney—who had struggled to have the court appoint her Gloria's legal guardian, really did take life by the steering wheel and—well, drive. Her aunt was almost, she supposed, the very opposite of her mother, who was, in a way, too much of a good thing. Her very sweetness and femininity, in the end, just seemed to play havoc with her: she became a sort of bauble in a world ruled by men.

The headlights of a passing car threw shadows across the living room ceiling, and the sound of a clock disappeared as it passed, only to recur again as the noise of the car gradually died away. Tick, tick, tick . . . She had no idea where the clock actually was.

Mrs. Whitney had wanted some kind of tradition and continuity in Gloria's life, and although Gloria loved her mother and always would, she couldn't help but be grateful, too, for her aunt's efforts at providing some sort of stability for her, although the custody trial had been an endless nightmare.

And then, of course, her aunt dared to make her own sculptures. And to have radical opinions about art. She simply had refused out of hand the traditional female role, and she had the nerve to take on the larger world of men, come what may. There really was some lesson of courage in her. She dared in a way Gloria couldn't help but acknowledge with admiration, and even gratitude.

Bill Saroyan, she knew, would probably not have pleased her aunt in the least (although there was a chance she might be susceptible to him because he was an artist). She smiled to herself in the dark, imagining the two confronting one another.

"Mr. Saroyan, I must ask you to lower your voice or leave my house at once."

What would Bill reply to such a request? Or would he simply throw a table at her? Would he turn into a beast before their very eyes and destroy a Picasso on the wall, knock over a Rodin sculpture and tell her aunt as it cracked into a thousand pieces, "Get lost"—?

Gloria suddenly realized her heart was racing; she was terrified. At the same time, she knew she had let her imagination get the better of her. Bill wasn't as heartless an ogre as *that*, now, was he? She supposed he couldn't be—an artist, after all—yet she still wasn't entirely convinced.

7

THE NEXT MORNING SHE WOKE UP EARLY, BEFORE CAROL, and gave Aram a bowl of Cream of Wheat. He ate most of it and then continued playing in his pajamas. The sky was an overcast gray again.

"Do you know how to make some of that coffee for me?"

"Arm grind coffee for Gloria," the little boy told her, going to a drawer in the kitchen for the coffee grinder and the beans.

By the time Carol shuffled out in her robe, smiling blearily and waving away her friend's smiling attention with the words "Don't look at me, darling, I'm a wreck," Gloria had eaten eggs and toast, had two cups of the very good coffee, and read an article in an old *Chronicle* about the buildup of Soviet power in Europe since the end of the war.

At the same time, she had come up with an idea, although she wasn't certain she could carry it through. Upstairs there were noises again: it seemed Bill had just gotten up too.

Carol had a cup of coffee, and they chatted aimlessly for a few minutes. Then Gloria decided to try her idea out loud, if only to see how it sounded.

"Darling, I'm going to go up to see Bill. I'm going to tell him that you're not mad at him anymore and that he should come down and—be with you and Aram."

Carol looked over at her friend with unfeigned awe.

"You're kidding?"

"No, I'm not—kidding. I mean I'm terrified, you know. Of course I am."

"Well, you're not as scared as I am. Oh, Gloria, why is it I have no guts at all—really none?"

"Carol," Gloria said, laughing and then catching her breath, "how can you say that? I mean I'm going to go upstairs, yes. I mean I hope I am, if I can keep up the nerve. But *you're* going to go on *living* with Bill. And I can tell you right now, I don't have *half* the courage for that."

Carol studied her friend.

"Gloria, I don't know what to say. Are you sure you want to climb those stairs and see that son of a bitch?"

"Well, look," Gloria said, laughing, "the worst he could do is hit me, and I figured out that wouldn't be *half* as bad as all the horrible things I can *imagine* him doing if I stay here like this much longer."

"You're positive?"

"I think so. Yes, I am. I'm going to go up there and just tell him."

"Oh, I'm so glad," Carol said suddenly with that pert, comic voice she used to switch conversational gears. Then she added: "But you've got to do me one very big favor. I mean *another* one."

"What?"

"You've got to wait till I get dressed and make myself very beautiful."

"Oh, but of course," she said, though Carol was looking absolutely ravishing, as always.

"Because let me tell you why. If he comes down here and I'm like this, he'll go *right back* upstairs. Believe me." Carol paused and then giggled.

"Well, darling," Gloria said smiling, "you look beautiful. But of course I'll wait."

"*Good.*"

Carol got up and walked toward the bathroom off Aram's room. She turned in the doorway of the kitchen and looked back at Gloria sitting at the kitchen table.

"Gloria, you're really a sensational friend: *the* all-time sensational friend. And if he does *anything* to you—anything at all—just yell and I'll run up and the two of us will beat him up."

Gloria started laughing, and then Carol started. But then Carol put her hand to her mouth quickly and pointed to the ceiling, afraid Bill might hear their unmuffled laughter.

8

AN HOUR LATER, GLORIA STOOD OUTSIDE THE FRONT door, which Carol held open from inside. There was no question of using the entrance to Bill's studio at the top of the stairs by the living room. When Gloria knocked, Bill would immediately suspect it was Carol, and even if Gloria were able to get this straightened out, the whole emotional impact of her being there would be lost. So she would go up the outside stairs and knock on his front door, as someone coming from the street would.

"Gloria," Carol whispered, as if she were afraid Bill might open his door and discover the two of them, "it's not too late to drop this whole thing, and come back in and be a sensible coward like me."

"Oh no. It'll be all right, you'll see."

"Now don't forget. If Bill does anything—I mean *any-thing*—scream and I'll be up with the big frying pan his mother gave me. It weighs four hundred pounds and I never realized what it was good for until now."

"Oh, no, sweetheart. Don't worry."

"All right, now I'm going to leave the door a little open so I can spy on you."

"Okay."

Gloria turned, swallowed, and began to walk up the stairs to Bill's door. The thirty-seven-year-old writer in his studio at the top of the stairs was in the midst of a crisis in both his life and his career. The Saroyan who dazzled the whole nation as a short story writer ("The Daring Young Man on the Flying Trapeze") and playwright *(The Time of Your Life)* during the Depression had, with the coming of the war years and the end of his youth, experienced a precipitous decline in the favor of critics and readers alike. The exuberant romantic who had been a literary hero a few short years before was now considered somewhat passé, and the publication of his war novel, *The Adventures of Wesley Jackson*, had been delayed for not being positive enough about the war effort. (Whereas *The Human Comedy*, the heartwarming home-front novel he'd written in 1943 before his own army experience, had been a huge success as both a book and an MGM movie starring Mickey Rooney.) In addition, he was now plagued by debts he had run up through compulsive gambling, and by his difficulties with Carol, now twenty-one years old and three months pregnant with their second child.

By the time she reached his landing, Gloria could feel her heart pulsing in her throat. Her whole body had broken into a sweat. Thank God for perfume.

On the other hand, it still wasn't too late to race down the stairs, hop into a cab, drive to the airport, and catch a plane to a foreign capital, somewhere like Paris, or maybe Cairo. And forget about everything here. She could phone Leopold en route and he would join her later. Yes, but Carol would be awfully bewildered and then sad to see her rush by her door. The whole thing was so crazy.

She knocked on Bill's unfinished wood door. She heard the rustling of a newspaper and then Bill's footfalls approaching the door. Then the door opened.

Bill had a couple of days' growth of beard but otherwise he looked much as she remembered him. He was wearing a Brooks Brothers striped shirt, open at the collar, and a pair of dark slacks. He was in his bare feet. He still had that look, a bit like Pat di Cicco's—like a handsome gangster.

He looked at her for a moment apparently without recognizing her, and then his face broke into a rather charming smile. "Gloria!" he said, as if they were old acquaintances who had surprised each other in a restaurant or a train station. "What are *you* doing here?"

"Well... Bill..." Gloria found herself both relieved and, having geared herself up for some sort of a struggle, disarmed enough to find it hard, for the moment, to make clear sense in English.

"Come on in, come on in," Bill said, waving her in through the door, which he now opened all the way. "So you came to see the kid, is that it?"

Well, *this* was Bill: "the kid." He wasn't referring to Aram.

"Sit down. Would you like some coffee?"

Gloria sat down on a black leather upholstered chair.

"Oh, no thanks," she said. "I've just really come to tell you that, that Carol—well, Bill, I'm sure *you know* she just loves you very, *very* much, and she's so sorry about what happened—and—and really, Bill. I mean the two of you belong together and I hope you'll—you'll just—come downstairs again. Because she loves you."

Standing in the center of the room, Bill put one bare foot on the seat of a wooden chair that had been painted bright red.

"Carol asked you to come up here and say that?" he asked Gloria in a much softer voice than he normally spoke in.

"Well, no, not exactly. I mean it was my idea, but it's what she feels... Bill."

For the moment, Gloria was too caught up in what she was doing to notice herself at all. Her fear had transformed itself into an act that involved only the recognition of each new moment's demand.

"I see, I see," he said. "Well, I appreciate your coming up here this way, Gloria. It's awfully nice of you to do that."

Bill was really something less, and something more, than the ogre she had been grappling with at the edge of all her thoughts for days. He was, rather, a medium-sized man, not terribly tall, who was obviously in the throes of his own troubles. But she'd only been able to see that by breaking through what it was that frightened her and coming up here into the light of day. She was suddenly so happy she felt like crying.

9

WHEN SHE LEFT BILL'S STUDIO AND WENT BACK DOWN-stairs to the landing, Carol opened the door before she could knock.

"I've been trying to hear but I couldn't make out any words."

"He's coming down. He really wasn't so bad. I think he was really sort of glad to have an excuse to stop this whole business."

"Come in, darling, come in."

Gloria went in, Carol closed the door, and the two walked into the kitchen. It looked as if it might rain again.

"Really?" Carol asked her. "Do you really think so?"

"Oh yes, darling. I think he's glad."

"Oh, Gloria, what an angel you are! Because he probably would've stayed up there for *years*, no matter what, if you hadn't gone up."

Bill was subdued when he came down a few minutes later. He said hello to Carol without kissing her, made an obviously perfunctory inquiry after Leopold to Gloria, and then immediately went into the kitchen to brew a pot of coffee. Gloria had an overwhelming sense that she was supposed to leave the house right away, that whatever was going to happen wouldn't happen until she was gone. She began to pack her things, and Carol, obviously anxious, helped, suddenly speaking in a whisper. She really *was* under a kind of spell when Bill was around.

Gloria made a reservation at the Fairmont and Carol called for a taxi for her. Then, when they heard the car's honk, the two women carried Gloria's bags downstairs themselves rather than disturb Bill, who was in the kitchen with Aram.

It was raining lightly now. Inside the taxi, Gloria rolled down the window while Carol stood distractedly on the sidewalk.

"You'll be at the Fairmont?"

"Yes."

"Well, I'll phone tomorrow."

"All right."

"Goodbye." Suddenly Carol came forward and the two hugged and kissed through the open window. "I love you, darling," Carol said. "You just saved my life. *Really.*"

10

GLORIA CHECKED INTO A ROOM ON THE FOURTEENTH floor of the Fairmont with a panoramic view of the city and the bay. Almost immediately she began trying to get a call through to Leopold at the number she had for the ranch. Somehow, the call couldn't be completed until seven that night. She sat on one of the twin beds with the curtains still open, though it had been dark outside for some time now.

"Beverly Crest," Leopold said. "You go to Beverly Crest, yes?"

"Well, I'll meet you there. I don't want to be in that big house all by myself." Leopold had just bought the house on Beverly Crest Drive in Beverly Hills and the idea of being in a house so huge and empty by herself was more than she could bear. "Leopold, how long—"

Suddenly the phone line seemed to be experiencing a tornado. Gloria stood up, catching sight of the city, twinkling below, through the window.

"Leopold?"

The phone line seemed to be engulfed by an unceasing chaos of air currents for the next twenty seconds, and then she heard Leopold's voice again, going along quite calmly.

". . . so Bill and Carol can have dinner with you?"

"No. I don't think so. Leopold, how long will it take you to get to Beverly Crest? I'll meet you there."

"Just a minute. I'll ask Tex."

As she held the phone, the line seemed to go into another storm, and then, abruptly, it grew quiet and calm. Leopold came on again.

"Tex says two days. That will be Saturday night."

"All right. Well, I'll take a train and meet you."

"Fine, my darling. Are you fine?"

"Oh, yes, sweetheart. I'm fine."

The next day, a partly cloudy one with the sun poking through at around three in the afternoon and making the city suddenly almost festive, Gloria spent walking around Union Square, window shopping.

San Francisco seemed to be a city of milder, almost pastel colors. The people had a slightly raw, open, easy-natured quality, that made them easily distinguishable from either New Yorkers or natives of Los Angeles. The trouble was— what was there to *do?* Unless, she supposed, you were married to a man like Bill who would make every day a marathon of charged emotions. He would certainly keep one busy. Poor

Carol, she thought, as she looked at some jade teacups on the third floor of Gump's. Perhaps, in the end, what she shared with Carol, and with Oona maybe too, was the fact that they were all, however differently, orphans. Was that the ineffable something in Carol's look that held her? It took an orphan, maybe, to recognize another orphan. And could it be that that was why all of them, now, happened to be married to world-famous artists much older than they were? Was there something in the combination of art with fame and power in these men that promised her and Oona and Carol the feeling of being taken care of that none of them had ever really known in childhood? Well, it sure looked like Bill, for one, was driving a hard bargain.

Late that afternoon she took a taxi to the Palace of the Legion of Honor and stood before Van Gogh's painting of his room in Arles, one of a collection in a traveling exhibition of Post-Impressionists.

On the wood floor of his room was a strange area of light that made it appear to be both the floor as it actually looked and at the same time as it looked specifically to Van Gogh alone. What a beautiful, mysterious thing that was! It was what she tried to do in her own painting—to make the color as specific as possible. If the color was exact, the subject could be done more broadly, suggestively—the way Milton Avery painted. And, of course, Matisse.

There were no messages for her late that afternoon when she got her key at the desk at the Fairmont, and bought a *Call Bulletin* at the newsstand in the lobby with the huge headline BLOODY REBELLION AT ALCATRAZ IS OVER. But when she opened the door to her room, there was a telegram lying on the floor just inside. She picked it up, wondering if it might be from Leopold. She would be leaving by train for Los Angeles early the next morning and meeting him at the house on Beverly Crest tomorrow night—unless there had been a change of plans.

It was twilight. Gloria walked over to the big window and

opened the telegram without turning on the lights. She unfolded the telegram and read it by the light from the window.

WE HAVE DECIDED TO CONTINUE OUR LIVES
TOGETHER AND TRY TO MAKEA FUTURE.
                    CAROL AND BILL

Gloria stood with the telegram in her hand, her eyes involuntarily rereading the message several times, and then studying the typographical error—"MAKEA"—as if it might impart the secret of such a fake and pompous and really absurdly impersonal telegram.

She knew immediately, of course, that Carol hadn't written it, but she couldn't help feeling a rush of anger in her blood that Carol hadn't intercepted this—this sort of *press release* communication. Really, Bill ought to have had more taste.

But then Gloria began to imagine what Carol might have wanted to write as a follow-up telegram—but never would have dared because Bill might catch her—and as she sat down in a chair by a little teakwood table in the slowly deepening darkness, she found herself laughing. Really, Carol was like some sort of strange, beautiful, and comic... divinity almost ... and if she couldn't always understand her, she would just have to take her on faith, she supposed. Maybe that's what friendship sometimes was.

PART TWO

Suddenly something flashed into her mind, so clear that it must have come from without, from the breathless quiet. What if—what if Life itself were the sweetheart? It was like a lover waiting for her in distant cities—across the sea; drawing her, enticing her, weaving a spell over her. She opened the window softly and knelt down beside it to breathe the cold air. She felt the snowflakes melt in her hair, on her hot cheeks. Oh, now she knew!

—Willa Cather, Lucy Gayheart

Suburban Snare
•
1953

1

I<small>T WAS ONE OF THOSE LATE SPRING EVENINGS IN</small> H<small>OL</small>-lywood when the light stays so long in the sky that it seems it may never get dark. And then you turn around and it's suddenly night. They were having dinner outside at the Beachcombers, six or seven people altogether, including Nick and Ruth Conte, who had arranged the evening. It was clear and warm, but the sound of a continuous, dripping rain came from the fountain—a lit-up deep-sea grotto, all electrified blues and greens.

Carol sat next to a young Englishman, Kenneth Tynan, who hardly said a word all evening. The theater critic for the London *Observer*, he had apparently come to town for the first time, and the Contes had met him and asked him to join their dinner party. She hardly knew any of the other guests either, but Ruth was darling, as always.

"I'm worried about you, Carol. You're not really cut out for the P.T.A., no matter what Bill might have in mind."

Carol had divorced Bill for the second time—their second marriage lasted only six months—and as a consequence of their divorce agreement she found herself with Aram and Lucy ensnared in a brand-new ranch house in a brand-new suburban development in Pacific Palisades.

"Oh, Ruth, I've got all the kids terrified on my morning for the car pool. They're so scared they don't talk. Aram and Lucy are very mad at me."

"You're not a morning person, Carol."

"No, I'm a night person and there *is* no night out here."

Everyone had laughed, but then, true to form, the dinner began breaking up at 9:45, everyone standing up beside the table, kissing and hugging goodbyes. Then, as she was walking into the parking lot, someone took her arm.

"Excuse me."

She turned and saw that it was the Englishman. He was very tall and had that sort of elegant, consumptive look of certain Englishmen. A very tall—wasn't it Keats?

"Yes?"

"Oh, I—I'd like to see you home. May I call a cab?"

"Oh, that's very sweet of you. But I have a car—I'm driving my ex-husband's old Cadillac."

A breeze full of ocean scents moved over them.

"Will you come to England and marry me?"

It was so abrupt she hardly had time to be startled.

"Oh, I don't think so. I can't even get to the drugstore."

"Oh, but you must. I've sat next to you all evening, and I'm absolutely and permanently under your spell. I'm in love with you and I want to marry you."

He seemed to be serious.

Carol felt suddenly as though the sea air contained some powerful pungency that had invaded her, upsetting her sense of balance. She steadied herself by putting a hand down on the trunk of one of those new Studebakers that looked like they could fly.

The Englishman smiled.

"Please. I have to go back to England tomorrow morning. Would you let me take you for a drink somewhere?"

"I can't. I've got a baby sitter; I have to let her go soon. If—" Carol hesitated.

"Please," he said, smiling and insistent, both.

"Well, you could come back to the house for a drink if you like."

"Oh, perfect."

• • •

She drove Bill's old gray tank of a Cadillac, taking Sunset into the Palisades. The Englishman asked to stop at a liquor store that was still open on Laurel, and returned with a bottle of wine. She drove back onto Sunset, already almost deserted.

"It *does* sort of shut off early around here, doesn't it?"

They went past the darkened Mayfair Market, where she usually shopped.

"Well, it's hard, in a way. Although I suppose it's wonderful for children and, of course"—Carol gave the line a certain emphasis, in case it had slipped his mind—"I do have two children."

Sometimes, at an evening with the Contes or at Dick and Jean Widmark's, it would occur to Carol that if someone should gaze into the living room window, she might appear to be the one of all the guests with the widest possible future. Here she was, still only twenty-eight, unattached, and everybody seemed to like her and care about her and find her pretty and funny. But the man at the window wouldn't know about Aram and Lucy. That was the difference. Unless of course that man was Bill. But then, who else would be spying on her? No, it was horrible, after all. Just horrible.

"I know you have children," the Englishman said. He had his window down and held his head back in the breeze. "You know, I'd want you to come and live with me in England, and the schools there really are the best in the world."

"You're not *still* . . ."

He sat up and turned to her. Carol kept her eyes on the road.

"You'll find, Saroyan, that I'm absolutely a man of my word. I find you divinely beautiful and witty, and I want to marry you."

She turned off Sunset onto Bienvenido, then took a right up Las Pulgas, which led into Maroney Lane, where Bill had put a down payment on the last house. There was a ranch where horses grazed just beyond the red reflectors on the backstop marking the dead-end road.

She pulled up into the driveway and turned off the engine. The crickets were going.

"How charming," he said, and got out with the bottle of wine. "Saroyan, this is the California I *wanted* to see."

Inside the brand new little ranch house, she paid Leslie, a pretty, dark-haired high school girl whose parents were English and lived farther up the hill on Las Pulgas, while Ken opened the bottle of wine in the kitchen.

"Sweetheart, what time did they get to bed?"

"Well, Lucy was asleep by eight, and Aram by eight-thirty or so."

"Ooo, Leslie, you're getting better with them than I am. Here, sweetheart."

"Oh, Mrs. Saroyan, you only owe me four dollars."

"That's nothing, darling—don't even talk about it. That's finished. Take it."

Bill, of course, would accuse her of every known self-delusion and depravity if he could see her giving the girl an extra dollar. But she had discovered that giving a tip, which she liked to do in any case, had its practical side. She could usually count on Leslie to work for her with only a couple of hours' notice.

She closed the front door and bolted the chain lock. Then she began her rounds. First she went to her bedroom at the far end of the house. She switched on the light and quickly got down on one knee to check for a man hiding under the bed. No one there—but it was important to *know* that.

She stood up again, quickly, turned off the light, and went into the little den with the picture window that turned into a black mirror at night. She switched the light on, checked the room over, and then caught sight of her own image in the window. When she switched the light off again, her image lingered on the air.

"How do you do? I'd like to marry you," she told her image out loud.

"Sorry, but that isn't possible," she answered herself. "You see, I've got two children and I'll never marry anyone again. I married a maniac *twice*, which means *I'm* crazy myself. Got it?"

"Saroyan, where are you?" Ken called from the living room. "And who are you talking to?"

She went back to the front foyer, and put her finger to her mouth before she opened Aram's door. Ken nodded that he understood to be quiet, and sat down on the living room sofa, holding a glass of wine. He had said he wanted to marry her. He was nuts, too—which was relaxing, in a way, even if it made his proposal less flattering.

She tiptoed into her nine-year-old son's room. He lay diagonally across his bed with his head in the corner, as though he had shot out from his covers but come up against a wall. His breathing, as she listened for a moment, was dense, as though he were in the thick of complicated life-dramas even while he slept. Then she covered him, tiptoed back out of the room, and closed the door.

"One more room," she whispered to Ken, as she crossed the foyer to go to Lucy's door.

The seven-year-old girl lay in her bed like a doll that had been put to bed by a particularly fastidious child. Her head was exactly centered on the pillow; her arms were over the blanket on each side of her in perfect symmetry. Carol leaned down to make sure she was breathing, although this was an almost nightly ritual and she was quite certain she was breathing. She leaned down rather just to listen a moment to the soft, delicious music itself. She got up, then, shut the door as she left the room, and walked out into the living room. The Englishman looked up at her with a smile.

"A glass of wine?"

"No thanks. I hardly ever drink."

"Will you sit beside me?"

"No. I don't understand you."

She sat down on the other end of the sofa, slipped off her shoes, and gathered her legs up under her skirt, Indian-style, facing him.

"That reminds me of a line by D. H. Lawrence. Do you like Lawrence?" he asked her.

"I've only read _Sons and Lovers_—in high school."

"Well, he wrote poetry, too. And there's a poem about fish. He says: 'I don't understand fish.' Isn't that marvelous? 'I don't understand fish.' I mean that's it, really, in a nutshell, isn't it?"

Perhaps he really _was_ crazy. She smiled politely, and as if catching her apprehensiveness, he continued on a more down-to-earth basis.

"But you must tell me about your life."

"I can't. There's nothing to tell. I have to drive the kids to school this morning."

She picked up a tangerine from the bowl on the coffee table and began to peel it, carefully placing the peels on a green china ashtray shaped like a big nasturtium leaf. Ken studied her, faintly smiling, and she continued.

"Other than that, I keep the house clean, and try to make decent dinners for the kids—and not commit suicide."

She had, in fact, enough sleeping pills in her medicine chest to kill herself.. She had gotten the bottle a few months before when it had suddenly dawned on her—with that strange relief that seemed to accompany even the most desolate coming to terms—that this was literally what she wanted to do. Sleep and never wake up.

Here she was, living in this middle-class suburban neighborhood, surrounded by perfect little families on every side. Eisenhower had defeated Stevenson to become President, and all was right with the world. Gloria was in New York. Oona was with Charlie in Switzerland—permanently it seemed. And she had nothing to live for, other than the children, and they would probably be better off with hired help.

Bill would come around in the evenings—at the time of
the divorce agreement he'd bought himself a small house on
stilts over the ocean at Malibu—and make her whore for any
household needs or slight luxuries that provided her mind an
occasional, momentary point of focus—the red stove she had
chosen for the kitchen, for instance. "A man has a need," he
would intone, keyed-up from his perennial working day at
the typewriter. Though the monthly child support checks
never seemed to arrive on time, he himself could be counted
on to put in an unscheduled appearance once or twice a week,
as often as not around the time the children were finally down
in their beds. And she was actually going to bed with him
again, with nothing in her heart but a kind of numb stupor.
She saw herself growing crude—out of a sense of complete
displacement and a boredom that seemed to crust over her
sense of utter failure and shame.

She had gone to bed the night after she bought the pills
with the idea that she would get the kids safely off to school
the next morning—and then take them. She knew that the
cleaning lady who came in once a week, a wizened middle-
aged black lady from Watts named Edwina, would find her
when she came in at noon, and so the kids would be spared
at least that level of the trauma.

But a funny thing had happened that morning. Just after
she woke up, while she was still lying in her bed, she began
to hear a woman shouting obscenities. She couldn't figure out
who it might be, or where it could be coming from. Her next-
door neighbors, the Ellerbys, were a quiet, model couple—
George was an engineer at Lockheed—with the slightly softer,
sweeter mannerisms Carol associated with the South. They
had two young daughters. It was inconceivable to her that
Helen Ellerby would actually raise her voice, let alone cut
loose in the style she was overhearing. She got up out of bed,
and went through the house in her nightgown, testing various
vantages for the loudness and clarity of the voice. She even
opened the front door slightly, standing behind it, to see if

the sound became any clearer. It was just after seven of a clear, fragrant May morning, already quite warm.

In the end, however, she returned to her pink bedroom, where the sound was clearest. And finally, she couldn't keep from looking out her window across the garden fence into what she knew would be George and Helen Ellerby's bedroom. Her access was embarrassingly perfect because their house was set at a slightly lower level than her own.

Now she saw Helen Ellerby standing stark naked—with a younger and fuller body than she would have guessed—in front of George and little Kathy and Gail, screaming bloody murder at them. Neither George nor the girls made any attempt at a reply, but rather stood—George in his pajamas, the two little girls in white flannel nightgowns with pink roses on them—in stunned, still sleep-bemused, silence.

"You all just go right ahead and fuck yourselves! You hear? The three of you, that's right. You think I like getting up every morning just to butter your toast? Well, I do not! No, I do not! That's right, fuck it!" It went on and on. Addressing George directly, she shouted, in a piercing octave: "Why, you dumb ox! Whoever *heard* of buttered home fries?"

Carol could barely believe her eyes and ears—the scene was so glorious a reassurance to her. Only out of the deepest inner propriety, combined with a sudden sense of female loyalty to Helen herself, did she finally tear herself from the window, put on her robe, and go to the kitchen to make breakfast for Aram and Lucy.

She burst into laughter as she filled a bowl with Rice Krispies and again, a few moments later, as she poured out a second cup of Minute Maid orange juice, but she stifled herself enough not to be noticed by the kids.

Accustomed, at that hour, to her at her most dour, they had long ago dropped any notion of conversation with her or even, for the most part, with each other, as they sat eating their breakfast at the sunlit table, a round white marble one she had found at Goodwill for twenty-five dollars.

By the time the kids were off to school, the episode was over. The Ellerby girls had gone off to school as well, and George to work in his blue Buick. Still, Carol found herself walking through the rooms of the little ranch house with a new feeling of lightness. Her heart all but overflowed with sympathy for Helen, and with admiration for the go-for-broke candor of her performance. In all her years with Bill, it was the thing she had never dared do, and yet maybe it was the one thing, finally, that might have worked. Well, that was pushing it—*nothing* would work, *ever*, with Bill. She knew that. That was the single deepest certainty of her life.

Yet having seen her next-door neighbor so nakedly allowed her to pull in her own horizons now, taking each day more on a moment-to-moment basis, while at the same time knowing that if it ever got too bad, she still had the option of the pills. And that made it easier in a way. Each night now, as she lay in bed just before falling into sleep, she could be conscious of the fact that she had gotten through one more day without doing what she had made it quite simple for herself to do.

"But you would never do that, would you?" Ken asked seriously.

"Well, I hope not." She smiled at him and then added, for the sake of pure mischief, "But I *might*."

"But you've everything ahead of you to look forward to." He was still apparently perfectly serious. Then, with a slight grin, he continued, "And I'm in absolute need of your company, till death do us part. You have no idea how beautiful you are, do you?"

"You're crazy," she answered, smiling. "I don't even know you."

Ken sighed deeply. "I know you're not anyone so ordinary as to say to a man who earnestly proposes marriage to you after spending two hours as your dinner partner, 'I don't even know you!' I'm convinced you're not like that at all. But not at all."

The crickets started up again in the back yard.

"Well, well, *well*..." Carol goaded him, her eyes steady.

"That's more like it," he said, taking this in his stride, smiling now. "The point is, I need you."

"Really? What for?"

For the next several hours, Ken proceeded to tell her something of his own life—an unhappy marriage he said he was in the midst of ending, his love of the theater and of the bullfights. He was a good talker, really a monologist, and it occurred to Carol suddenly that she was in the presence of another writer—by itself a rather gruesome thought. But there was something reassuring about the way Ken Tynan threw caution to the winds, deciding he had to marry her (no ifs, ands, or buts) before they had exchanged two words. Even if it were all a high-flown performance on his part, as seemed to her entirely probable, it nevertheless had taken a certain generosity of spirit—whereas Bill's deepest quality, and the one she had come most deeply to detest, was a self-protective caution with regard to everyone and everything that, in the end, made him into a full-fledged spiritual and emotional miser.

Bill was one of those writers who would end up resenting you if he wanted to sleep with you and you went ahead and went to bed with him, because after all was said and done he really believed that it had sapped him of his creative juices. So you were put in that position of being a loathsome horror no matter what you did. And, in essence, this was true of *all* his relationships. "He has a face like a sexual organ," he would say suddenly but offhandedly of someone they had spoken cordially with at a party. To Carol, there was something deeply unsettling—as if it were traitorous to the whole human race—in even being privy to such a comment.

So it was a relief to see a writer like Ken, whatever his work might or might not be worth—she would have to read it— who preserved some of the larger human decencies. Jim Agee, she supposed, was like that, too; and, of course, Truman was—and they were both marvelous writers. But in the end, the work hardly mattered, really, unless you actually were ready to value art over life, which was probably *the* most romantic and disastrous notion anybody could ever get stuck with, as she herself was a sort of living proof. For she wondered from time to time if it hadn't been precisely Bill's way of speaking to her when he wanted to be romantic—"You're like after the rain," he had told her once—that had gotten to her so disastrously.

"I just realized—" Ken broke off suddenly. "I just realized my plane's at eight this morning."

"Well, it's too late now for me to go to bed. It'll be light soon. Would you like some coffee?"

"Coffee would be great in a minute."

Ken got up and went to the sliding picture-window doors that led from the living room to a cement patio in the backyard.

"Saroyan, will you come out here with me?"

He slid the glass-paneled door open, and walked onto the patio with a hand trailing in back of him for Carol. She followed him, without taking his hand, in her bare feet.

The backyard was small, and bordered by an embankment that rose fifteen feet or so and supported a stand of eucalyptus trees. There was a pinkish dawn light through the trees at the top of the embankment, and the air was quite cool and full of the sharp fragrance of the eucalyptus. The patio was wet with dew—a chill, bracing sensation Carol rather liked.

Ken towered over her, and he put his arm around her without looking down at her.

"Life is sort of a sad lark, isn't it, Saroyan? Up and down, in and out—and a bit over-complicated now with all these jets. It was easier for my English ancestors. A bit of humble porridge keeps a man's head in place. I devoutly hope I don't go down in a wreck today...."

"Oh, you won't, Ken. I'm sure you won't."

"If I do, would you miss me just the tiniest bit?"

"Well, of course, I would."

"Saroyan, would you let me kiss you?" He turned down toward her now, his features only vaguely discernible in the still-dark morning.

She really didn't know who Ken Tynan might be, beyond the flamboyant romantic he seemed to like to play.

"Well—" she hesitated, "I guess that would be all right."

He kissed her well, lingeringly. For just the briefest instant, she was involved in the kiss, but then he moved his head away.

"I do want you to come to England and marry me."

"Yes," she said softly, "I know."

"Will you, then?"

"I don't think I'm the kind of person who should get married."

"Neither am I," Ken said, and sighed another deep sigh. "But I believe that once you take the vows, you really ought to hold to them."

A sparrow made a single chirp from the eucalyptus stand. "Oh, yes."

"And I believe I could honor those vows if I were married to you, Saroyan."

"You do?"

"Yes, my sweet. I think so."

He kissed her once more, rather lightly, and they went indoors again and Ken called a cab while she made a pot of coffee. By the time the taxi arrived, it was light outside, one of those white mornings when the sky seems very low. After saying goodbye, Carol stood waving to Ken from the driveway and then, when the car had disappeared, breathed deeply a few times in the dew-heavy, geranium-scented air.

2

KEN BEGAN WRITING IMMEDIATELY. "YOU HAVE BURNED deep into my bone marrow. I am helplessly—hopelessly—in love." Carol answered the first two or three of these letters but then couldn't keep up. He was quite mad. For one thing, as far as she knew, he was still married. Yet there had to be, after all, at least for her, a certain unavoidable charm about him, too. She wasn't *that* strong—and was anybody? Not to be affected just the slightest little bit by such vivid, intensely romantic attentions? Underneath everything, it was true, he probably really wasn't her type at all—although, on the other hand, it was hard to be too definite about that since she had really never met anyone even remotely like him.

A little more than a year after their first meeting, during the summer of 1954, Carol went to Europe. At the last minute, she took Aram and Lucy too. Bill had canceled out on his commitment to take the kids for the summer—to which he was bound by their divorce agreement—but to fight him was to lose half the battle at the outset. So, rather than give up the trip she had planned (Bill's underlying idea, she was certain, in canceling), she decided to take the kids and see if she could make up the extra money that would be needed while she was in Europe. She might even be able to get a few acting jobs; she knew enough people in the business so that there were a few possibilities. It might also be fun.

She went to Geneva, Switzerland, first, where her sister, Elinor, had taken a house with her two young children, Hubert and Anne, by her ex-husband, the titled but not wealthy Frenchman, Baron Henri de la Boullerie. At the same time, the beautiful, rather melancholic young English film star Kay Kendall arrived for a visit to Elinor's, and she and Carol struck up an instantaneous friendship, each a single woman, each, in her way, an "original." They took to calling each other "wifey." To help Carol out, Oona invited Aram to come and stay with the family in Vevey, where he would be able to play with his friends from before the Chaplins' American exile, Michael and Geraldine. And Elinor said she would be happy to have Lucy stay with her.

With the children settled for now, Carol and Kay Kendall went to London, where Carol got some voice-over work, dubbing in the English for the heroine of an exportable Italian romantic comedy. She made quite a bit of money. Then Marian and Irwin Shaw, whom she had run into at a London party, invited her for a weekend at their summer house on the coast of Spain. The house turned out to be marvelous— a villa overlooking the harbor. The Shaws were old and dear friends—Irwin had been in the same Film Unit with Bill in London during the war. They never discussed Bill, of course, yet she sat helplessly on the sunny terrace on Saturday morning over coffee, as an old story played at the borders of her conscious thoughts.

It was during the war, after Bill had been shipped overseas, and she lived in a sort of continual mourning for him through all the lonely days and nights. Still riding the crest of Bill's success, they were living then in the penthouse apartment at Two Sutton Place South; and she would carry Aram, not yet a year old, out onto the terrace at night and look at the East River. "At least we're facing in the right direction, sweetheart," she would tell the baby, "where your papa is, across the ocean."

Then Oona and Charlie arrived in New York from California and took a suite at the Plaza, and it was so much fun seeing them again—really for the first time since she and Oona had both gotten married—she almost forgot her constant sense of sorrow, of stomach-churning loss. Chaplin liked to have lunch at "21" with business associates, accountants, and his lawyer. At the same time, Oona and Carol would eat at the next table and talk, trying to catch up on everything that had happened since they'd both married. Oona was close to term now with Geraldine.

At one lunch they invited an acquaintance of theirs from the period before their marriages. She was a petite, very attractive brunette, and they were both looking forward to seeing her again because there would be so much gossip. Their friend had had affairs with most of the big names in Hollywood and New York, and as their lunch progressed the two wasted no time getting on the subject, about which their guest showed no noticeable reticence.

"What about Tyrone Power?" Carol asked her at one point.
"Yes."
"*Really?* Oh my God."
"And was he—"
"Wonderful."
"And Errol, of course," Oona interjected.
"Of course."
"Well—" Carol paused for a moment, sorting.
"John Garfield?" Oona asked in the interim.
"Uh-hunh."
It was sort of staggering, really. There just didn't seem to be anyone she had missed—other than a few who didn't really matter anyway. She was quite amazing—and she really was pretty, and quite smart. She had a kind of street smarts, Carol supposed. Eventually, perhaps in an effort to glean some lesson from what amounted to a sort of embarrassment of riches, Carol posed the ultimate question.

"Well, all right," she said, "of all of them—absolutely everyone—who was the best?"

Without the slightest hesitation, lifting her knife and fork in a sort of spontaneous tribute, she replied, "Irwin Shaw."

"Really?" Carol and Oona echoed one another, riveted. "Why?"

"I don't know," she answered. "There was just something about him. It was before his marriage, of course."

Several years later, when Carol got around to telling Irwin this story, she added, just for fun: "And Irwin, I've told this story to absolutely *everyone*, so I'm sure I'm responsible for some of your best and happiest times."

But then, that afternoon at "21," the inevitable *next* question had come up.

"And who," Oona asked, with a sudden gleam in her eye, "was the worst?"

"I can't tell you," their guest replied flatly.

Carol and Oona were not about to be deterred by any last-minute and, under the circumstances, entirely inappropriate scruples.

"Oh, *please*. Please tell us." By begging so flagrantly, Carol thought she could kid her out of her sudden, almost pathetic sense of propriety, like someone naked trying to hide behind a Band-Aid.

"I can't. I'm sorry. I just can't."

It was as if, having completely forgotten herself and betrayed the deepest secrets of her life, the poor girl now suddenly remembered that she was supposed to be someone else—someone, perhaps, with aristocratic reticence. Sad.

"But you *must*," Oona said, smiling. "We'll die if we don't find out. And Carol, we promise not to tell *anybody—ever*. Right, darling?"

"Oh, yes," Carol said. "Please. Nothing will ever leave this table, but we absolutely must know. Darling, we promise."

"We *do*," Oona underlined again.

"Well, if you really insist then," their guest answered finally, looking beyond them at the wall. "It was—Bill. It was Bill Saroyan."

Carol had some food in her mouth, but swallowing didn't seem to be a possibility. She kept her head down for the moment, and tried to restore a breathing pattern that would allow the food to go down. She was suddenly hot, flushed. She noticed, too, that Oona wasn't saying anything. Finally, she managed to swallow, and looked up.

"Oh, but that's not true," she said earnestly.

"I'm sorry," said their guest with all sorts of fake compassion in her eyes. "But you insisted."

Carol had a strong impulse to strangle her right on the spot.

"Oh, but Oona," she said, turning to her friend. "It's absolutely not true. Oona, I swear to you." She could barely keep herself from saying that Bill had probably just loathed her, that was all.

"Oh, of course, darling," Oona said to her. "Oh, I know."

But she probably had her doubts. "Oona, Bill is a *wonderful* lover. He's absolutely superb. I swear to you. I mean I want you to sleep with him, darling, so you'll know."

Oona started laughing, and so did the little horror—who, it turned out, when Carol had had a few more years to consider the matter more thoroughly, was probably not that far off the mark. Well, it was true that a few years after the incident she learned from Bill that, before meeting Carol, he'd had a rather serious affair with this woman. In light of this, her behavior at lunch might be taken for no more than elaborately contrived sour grapes. The little bitch. But still, Bill didn't, properly speaking, make love at all. Rather, he became possessed by desire—in fact, he seemed never *not* to be possessed by it when he was around Carol—and he never really gave much time or thought to any of the so-called finer points when he went about satisfying his desire. While she was still really a girl, this hadn't mattered much to her. There had been, rather, something thrilling about having a man so obviously passionately involved with her. Only a few months after the lunch, however, while Bill was still overseas, Carol got her first serious inkling that Bill might have had a few things to learn in that department, when she discovered an old marriage manual left by previous tenants on the top shelf of one of the kitchen cupboards and learned that there was such a thing as a "female orgasm." Alone one afternoon in the living room while Aram took his nap, she found herself growing hot with embarrassment, and then sudden anger. How could Bill either not know or not care about something as important as this?

That afternoon the Shaws took her to an outdoor luncheon at a hotel on the plaza in San Sebastián, and the table, it turned out, included both Ken Tynan and his wife, Elaine. Under the circumstances, Carol was more subdued than she ordinarily might have been, her eyes gravitating out toward the sailboats on the bay, studying the pattern the sunlight would strike into each particular sail. It was a lovely day, full of the smell of Spain, and the sea.

In Paris, on a lark, she had dyed her blond hair jet black, and for a moment she considered the possibility that in doing so she had upset Ken Tynan's romantic apple cart; but then, suddenly he had pulled a chair up beside her chair.

"Saroyan," he whispered to her, "will you get up with me right now and walk away from this?"

"No—I won't," she whispered back. He really was out of his mind.

"I want you to get up and come away and marry me. Do it right now."

"No...I don't want to do that."

Finally, he had returned to his chair beside his wife, and it seemed to Carol that now, perhaps, his fervor would end. It wasn't that, in certain situations, she couldn't imagine herself complying in adultery, it was just that, with Ken, there was something fundamentally wrong—or, perhaps, just unserious—about the whole thing from the beginning. She liked him. He was sweet and flattering. But that was really it. Period. And that would have to be clear to him now too.

3

BUT IT WASN'T. BECAUSE WHEN SHE AND THE KIDS RE-
turned from Europe to the Palisades, there was a whole slew
of new letters from Ken, as fervent, or more so, than the
earlier ones. "You are as mysterious and magnetic as high noon
on the Nile. Or midnight." Obviously her hair had made at
least a subliminal impression. If she appeared at their next
chance meeting in blackface, would a whole new gamut of
metaphors be called up? Was he warming up for his drama
reviews, or what? It was really an almost purely epistolary
love affair, at least on his part: nouns and verbs and adjectives
all tumbling into romantic juxtapositions, endlessly and forever. He just wouldn't stop. But she had stopped, and she
wasn't going to start again. Nevertheless, the mail did offer
a little distraction, here in her suburban snare again.

The red stove in the afternoon sunlight. Hello, hello, hello.
Aram's room, Lucy's room, her room. The den, with those
Matthew Barnes paintings (the best paintings Bill had ever
bought—he usually preferred paintings he could look down
on, as it were) of a lonely little figure of a man trudging from
the lower corner of the canvas toward some gloomily lit haven
in an otherwise overwhelming, abysmal night. Her life? Except for the haven, perhaps. Unless it was this den itself,
which now, with the kids back in school, became her favorite
room. It was, precisely, nowhere. And if she drew the curtains
and turned on the lights—as she liked to do—it was no time,
too. Or rather that particular, vaguely peopled midnight she

knew to be her own mind, day in and day out, whether she happened to be in Paris or the Palisades.

Now, in the late mornings, after a breakfast of black coffee—she would return to bed for several hours after the kids left for school—Carol would lock all the doors in the house and go back to the dark den. Here, she would turn on the lights and sit down at a pitted oak desk Bill had bought when they had lived on West Fifty-eighth Street, near the Plaza Hotel, just before their first divorce. She had a yellow legal-sized lined pad, and lots of highly sharpened pencils—she kept a schoolchild's little blue plastic pencil sharpener in her desk drawer—and she began to write.

Here, in this room, nowhere in no time, she would remember and write about other rooms, all those first rooms of her life, of the first breaking light of her mind and memory as a foster child. Her whole early life was a succession of those rooms—or rather of bureaus, bed tables, beds, and upholstered chairs. She remembered watching sunlight move across a wall, over a yellow painting of the baby Jesus, and then beyond. The story of her early childhood was like some long dream of weather witnessed in a room: one night—she must have been three or four—a full moon, huge and almost human, at the window.

Then school: a slow-healing scratch on her knee; the smell of books and ink; middle-aged women teachers with leaden perfumes that spoke of dense biographies in other, gloomy rooms. "Hey, buddy, can you spare a dime?" The Depression was a national hit, so to speak, everybody moving around to the same tune. Her mother gave the people who took her in some of the little money she made as a millinery model at Macy's. This, so they could feed her, and dress her, and she could go to school and learn to read and to write, and to add and subtract.

A thirtyish, rather stout Catholic woman in Paterson, New Jersey, Genevieve Laragay, became her final, long-term foster parent. She taught her to say the Hail Mary. She gave her

her own maroon towel and wash cloth and sometimes at night she read her fairy tales from the *Blue* and *Red Fairy Books*.

When her mother came to visit, everything went faster inside her. She was full of a breathless gaiety that made Carol's heart race. Then, after she had gone, and the rooms once more assumed their staid, domesticated gray, Carol felt half of herself tangled up in space somewhere, a deep pit of longing opened in her for whatever part of herself was missing. Where her father was, or even *who* he was, was something she didn't even dare to ask.

And so her room, her bed, her bureau, her little oxfords, her pillow, her glass, and her green toothbrush—the whole external kit of herself—became terribly important. Because when her mother went away, it was as if these were what was left of Carol. They were the pieces of a puzzle she could slowly assemble into herself again. And she would become terribly slow now, just looking, barely breathing—as before, during her mother's visit, she had gulped—trying to find her own face again, the look she had, the mind she had, before her mother had come.

Now the days went into her in the pattern they had, the school so large in it, until gradually she would be what she was, what the pattern would make of her, again. She was learning—she was reading by herself the little book her mother had left for her, *Honeybunch and Her First Garden*, before she went to bed. Then she would lay the book down on the bed table, turn the light off, and, kneeling at the end of her bed in the darkness, say her prayers.

The day her mother took her back with her to an eighteen-room apartment with eight servants at 420 Park Avenue, it was as if, at eight years old, she had suddenly exchanged lives, been given another autobiography. Manhattan seemed to have the clearest, sharpest light in the world, and her eyes began to work diligently in this extraordinary field of vision. Somehow, again, she might be able to pin herself down by what she saw—but this time the spectacle was vast and dazzling.

Her poor mother, the millinery model, had married a rich older man, Charles Marcus, a scientist and the vice president of Bendix Aviation. She was suddenly living like a queen, and set Carol up in her own bedroom—with a chandelier in it—like a little princess. They would ring for a servant any time they wanted something to eat or drink. Sometimes, addressing the help or some venerable guest of her husband, her mother affected an English accent, as if she, too, had exchanged life stories. She was no longer a Russian Jewish immigrant's daughter, but a member of the British aristocracy. She had invented herself, and Carol, if she liked, could follow her clues. On the other hand, there was Daddy.

She remembered a sitting room she had shared with him in Berlin just before the war. He was on a business trip for Bendix and had taken her with him, but it was hard for him to maintain his work schedule and at the same time keep her entertained. She remembered looking out their hotel window and seeing German soldiers marching in the street below. She would go away for a while and then come back to the window, and there they would be again, still marching. She imagined they were marching around and around the block. It was only near the end of their stay that it occurred to her, with a touch of wonder and then a sudden chill of fear, that the soldiers were not marching around the block; they were just—hundreds upon hundreds, thousands upon thousands of them—marching past the hotel window.

Daddy had been genuinely sweet with her during that trip. It was 1936 and she was eleven. He had hired a middle-aged German lady to baby-sit her while he went off to work, but she couldn't remember doing anything except looking out the window at the endless soldiers. They kept coming and coming and coming. One night at dinner, he apparently noticed her mood and asked her how she was feeling.

"I think I'm homesick."

He took this in, nodding seriously, and then answered, "I am too. I miss Marian."

Marian was their chambermaid in New York—a very sweet middle-aged woman, but so incredibly dumb that there were all sorts of little jokes about her in the house. She seemed to lose her mind as she walked from one room to another, so that it was important to ask her to do something in the same room where she was to do it. Writing things down might have been a solution except that Marian, who was Danish, had never learned to read and write English. Yet she was wonderfully clean and hard-working and good spirited.

"Yes," he told her, "I'm homesick too. I miss Marian very, very much."

This made Carol suddenly giggle, and then, when a smile began to play around the corners of Daddy's lips, laugh and laugh. A few days later they went on to Italy and the trip got much better. Thank God for the strange, shy man who had saved her life.

For it was he who recognized that though she shared her mother's striking blond beauty, Carol's mind was very much her own: full of comic sharp corners, hairpin turns, slapstick reversals, and madcap rebuttals. At Dalton, she was a good student and was liked—but also, among her all-female classmates, thought somewhat haughty, and just the slightest bit feared. What made her friendships with Oona and Gloria so special was that they were absolutely without female jealousy—and when she would encounter this with other girlfriends she would be surprised and disappointed. Oona O'Neill, whom she met at one of the first cotillions she attended and who became her closest friend, was the first person she ran into who seemed to share her own speed: Oona's home broken but her name itself fabled, famous. The two girls discovered they could eat whole hamburgers in just over two minutes at Hamburger Heaven on Madison Avenue at Sixty-seventh Street. Each of them, too, shared a fundamental sense of urgency and seriousness that made almost everything funny.

And then, of course, there was the business of their not really having known their fathers.

Then, when she met Gloria Vanderbilt, Carol felt as if her own—as opposed to her mother's—life was finding its own worldly sphere. Here was Gloria, whom she'd read about for years in the columns, liking her and wanting to be her friend. Carol reached into these friendships, in fact, with a kind of intensity and velocity that betrayed her own wariness within her mother's new life, as though it might at any moment prove to be only a short-lived sleight of hand. There was the winter evening Gloria phoned from her mother's house in Beverly Hills to ask her to be a bridesmaid at her wedding to Pat di Cicco. Carol was seventeen and had graduated the previous June from Dalton. They had been at dinner, but when her mother heard it was Miss Vanderbilt, she allowed Carol to take the call in her room.

"I want you to be a bridesmaid, darling—would you?"

"Would I? Would I? My God, I'd be thrilled!"

Late that December, after Pearl Harbor happened and her scheduled coming-out party was canceled along with everyone else's, Carol took a plane with Gloria's mother and her aunt Thelma to Los Angeles, and stayed with them in their house on Maple Drive in Beverly Hills during all the parties and events before and after the wedding in Santa Barbara.

The night of Gloria's call, when she came back to the dinner table and answered her mother's questions—watching her mother virtually swoon with the same kind of excitement she herself felt—it was as though her adult life had now, officially, begun. She resolved to speak less intimately to her mother from now on; she wanted to protect both Gloria and Oona from any outside scrutiny. For these two friendships had begun to deliver her into a world of her own, in which her mother's solicitude and protection would no longer be so important to her.

•   •   •

Then, one night before she returned from California to New York, at Musso Frank's in Hollywood, Artie Shaw—whom Carol knew because he was a friend of the singer Lee Wiley, who was a close friend of her mother's—introduced her to Bill Saroyan. She had played a small role in a production of his play *Jim Dandy* at Princeton that fall. And suddenly this man, who she assumed would be much older than she was, appeared. And it was all over.

He *was* older, but not old. He was a man, like Pat di Cicco was. He made no secret of the fact that he wanted to sleep with her. Artie, whom she had had a real crush on up to that moment, was too much of a gentleman to take her seriously. She was just seventeen. But Bill apparently wanted to get into her pants the moment he saw her. There was an urgency in him, a racing wit; he seemed to be sweating with his big-time life and fame—laughing louder than anybody else, telling the funniest stories.

The minute he had her alone in his hotel room, which was the same night they met (because, she knew now, she had been crazy, in a kind of mad panic to ruin her life, to go back to hell), he wanted to get her into bed. That she was an under-aged virgin meant absolutely nothing to him. He told her she was like fields of wheat in sunlight. He told her she was like vanilla ice cream and pink rose petals. Then, for the first time in her life, she was lying in bed with a grown man. The lights were off. It was a mild night, and Bill kept the window open so there were occasional noises of the traffic off Hollywood Boulevard. There was a sort of roar under it all, she remembered: the roar of Hollywood, or life, or Bill—that roar before her whole being was devoured for years.

Yet, there had been *one* moment. It was in the elevator at the hotel he stayed at, the Hollywood Knickerbocker. They had been together once or twice now without having gone all the way and he was going to drive her home, and she saw his face—just for a split second—and thought to herself, Well, he might not be such a nice man and maybe I shouldn't see him again. It had actually passed through her mind—the whole thought, one full turn—and at the very beginning. But then she was gone.

It was strange, too, because he frightened her from the beginning. For if Oona and Gloria and she seemed to share the same speed, Bill, when he wasn't languishing in his bed for days on end to recover his momentum, was actually *faster*. If she knew a certain easy wit in herself, at least in the proper surroundings, Bill had it in spades. Later she would know how much his work was all a sort of literary matinee idol's turn, full of tried and true effects, his proven bag of tricks (she couldn't read the words "swift" or "courteous" in his work now without practically puking), but at the same time, he knew how to dazzle with words.

One night, Jim Agee, whom she met originally at the Chaplins' before their move to Vevey, came over to the Maroney Lane house, and she worked up the courage to read to him from her pages, the pages she had been writing all about her child-hood without quite knowing what they were or why she was writing them. He was wonderful about it. He told her he loved what she was writing, and there was no condescension— as she knew she would encounter with Bill—in anything he said. He told her it was a book she was writing; in fact he even called it a novel.

Then he came over again one night and read to her from something he was working on about the end of his marriage, a piece called "Bigger Than We Are" that was the best thing she had ever heard about a real marriage. After that, he would stop by from time to time in the evenings. After a discussion of the joys of Mozart, he returned on another evening having in the meantime memorized an entire piano concerto. He then proceeded to play it on the living room piano for Carol: a performance that had the poetic poignancy of a huge, dogged devotion not quite equal to the task.

He was a writer obviously so different from Bill. He listened to her as well as speaking himself, shaping his talk with his large hands, smoking, drinking—another night person, on the wrong side of the continent. His conversational moon came out after midnight, the same as her own. He had already had several heart attacks and was only in his early forties. At first she had been afraid Bill might arrive on one of his unannounced evening visits and discover them. But Jim wasn't bothered. "You're afraid of Saroyan," he told her. "I'm not."

4

IT WAS LATE FALL NOW, THOUGH THE CALIFORNIA DAYS scarcely betrayed the seasons. There was more rain, but for the most part it was mild, balmy rain, and the sky would be clear the next day and all the fragrances would be sharper. Gloria came out to visit for a few days, and Carol made a bouquet of daisies and roses from the garden and put them in the den where Gloria slept on the foldaway couch. There was some tension between her and Leopold but Gloria didn't ever say much about that sort of thing. Had she come out to get away from the marriage? It was maddening really: she would never say just what was going on. And she now had two sons, Stan and Chris, with Leopold.

On Gloria's last night there, the two gave a party together. Carol took care of the garnishes, and Gloria was bartender. They served a big ham and had May wine. Their guests began arriving around seven-thirty, and Aram and Lucy were allowed to circulate for a while before going to their rooms and to bed. It was a real mix of her friends and Bill's, people met at the Chaplins' and elsewhere, who were still her friends, she was reassured to discover, after she and Bill split up. The Contes came, Gene and Betsy Kelly, John and Joan Houseman, Norman and Peggy Lloyd, the Widmarks, Ross and Armen Bagdasarian, and Ollie Carey.

Carol rushed around to make sure everyone had a drink or food. She was always on duty at her own parties, to a degree that made it hard for her to enjoy them.

"Carol, sit down," Jean Widmark told her firmly, smiling, sitting at one end of the sofa.

"I can't, Jean," Carol answered with a breathless little-girl voice. "I have to make sure the party is a big, *big* success!"

"But Carol..." Jean laughed.

"Oh, Jean," Carol replied, "don't *be* like that. You know how I hate parties."

Jean laughed again, surrendering affectionately to the non sequitur. Across the room, her husband's laughter, the most sinister in motion picture history, sounded for the third or fourth time that evening, in this context a wonderful reassurance. John Houseman had just speculated about the quality of any wine that would actually pay to advertise—as a California brand was currently doing on national television—only the red seal it used over its cork. A little while earlier, someone had put a Lena Horne record on Carol's little portable high-fidelity phonograph.

All of a sudden, it was eleven o'clock. All the food had been eaten, everyone was holding a drink, everyone was talking, Lena Horne was singing, and nobody seemed even remotely on the verge of leaving. This was not the usual evening in Los Angeles. The party had "taken," like a piece of music; and now it had its own time.

By one in the morning, Carol realized that they might be in the midst of setting some sort of local record. Nobody even looked up when she surveyed the room, standing beside the dinner table in the little alcove beside the kitchen.

Gloria and Carol made scrambled eggs and a pot of coffee for everyone at around four in the morning, and, after eating, the guests now reluctantly began to take their leave.

"Don't you ever do this again," Dick Widmark teased Carol affectionately at the door. Then she waited for his inevitable last line: "See you later," he said.

"Give me an hour, will you?" Carol joked.

"Now, *Carol*," Jean breezily interceded.

Dick laughed his mad killer laugh out in the dew-touched dark of the driveway.

"I like your friend," Jean added after a moment.

"Isn't she sweet?" Carol said, standing with Gloria in the light of the doorway.

"She's *adorable*," Armen called as she got into Ross's MG. "Call me, darling."

"Oh, I will," Carol said.

"Bedtime!" Ollie Carey yelled, repeating her den mother's line in John Ford's *The Searchers* and giving everyone a final laugh.

By the time they closed the door a gray dawn light was breaking.

"Carol," Gloria told her, "go to bed. We'll clean up in the morning after the kids go to school."

Carol woke up at eleven-thirty. It was a warm, sunny day and her room was suffused with its pink, peaceful light. But her alarm hadn't gone off and now the kids would miss a day of school. She put on her robe and slippers and walked out to the living room. Gloria was sitting on the sofa reading the morning L.A. *Times*, which Carol had started to have delivered to keep up with the McCarthy hearings, which she also sometimes watched on television in the afternoon. It took Carol a moment before she realized that everything from the night before had been cleared away. The house looked immaculate. And someone had gotten the kids off to school too.

"My God, how did you do it?"

"Sweetheart, it was just some plates and glasses."

Later that afternoon, Carol noticed that in the kitchen trash basket there were two gin bottles, while there was still half to three-quarters left of the vermouth they'd bought. So, that was how Gloria had done it: she spiked the drinks, and the party took off. She had such know-how—and such sweetness. Carol realized how much she'd missed her.

"I discovered your secret," she told Gloria as they sat over coffee at the dining room table. "All-gin martinis. Everyone got plastered."

"Well, you did too, didn't you?" she answered, smiling, obviously delighted herself with the success of the party.

"You know I never drink—especially at my own party. Gloria, I don't think you realize we just set a record. Everyone is home and in bed *asleep* in this town by eleven-thirty at the latest."

"Oh, Carol, I'm going to miss you."

She drove Gloria to the airport that evening after giving the kids their dinner. Leslie came over to babysit. It was twilight along the Pacific Coast Highway; the palm trees waved their arms like very tall sentries. Or, she supposed, lifeguards. Carol had a lump in her throat.

Gloria said, "What will it take to get you back to New York, where you belong? Would a thousand a month do it? Because you've got it."

Suddenly she wanted it more than she would allow herself to feel. Maybe because Gloria always seemed so much in control of her own destiny, the possibility of taking hold of her own life again—or really for the first time—became real to her for a moment. But she knew that ever since Gloria had come into her four-million-dollar inheritance at twenty-one, people were continually asking her for favors. The same, of course, was true for Oona after she married Charlie. There were demands on them from every possible corner. And part of their friendship, for Carol, was their implicit trust that she would never use them in such a way.

"Oh, I'd love to go to New York," she told Gloria as they passed the Santa Monica pier, the sun spots dancing on the water, "and I *will*. You'll see. It'll just be a little while, too. I can't go on like this, I know that, but I want to work it out on my own. But it's so sweet of you to offer that."

"Darling, you can pay me back when you get on your feet."

By the time they got to the airport, it was dark. Carol pulled up beside the American Airlines terminal and leaned across her seat to kiss Gloria. Both of them said a red-eyed, muffled goodbye.

O'Sullivan in Spain
1955

1

A MONTH LATER, EARLY IN DECEMBER, BILL ARRIVED ONE night and told her that the City Center in New York wanted to stage a revival of *The Time of Your Life*. He was obviously excited about it, more relaxed and positive than she'd seen him in months, wearing a bright red crewneck sweater, but it wasn't something she herself could be expected to be terribly thrilled by. She supposed it meant she was going to sleep with him to celebrate, but she stayed in the kitchen, finishing the dinner dishes, while he paced around.

"You don't get it, do you, kid?"

"What do you mean, Bill?"

"Well, I thought you were an actress. Are you an actress, or what?"

She turned from the dishes and looked at him, holding a towel to her hands.

"What are you talking about?"

"Take it easy, take it easy," he said, smiling and turning next to the stove to face her. "I'm talking about Mary L., that's what I'm talking about. Your hair's the right color now, and if you *are* an actress, as you *say* you are ... or is that just talk, the big telephone-call confidence you put most of your life into?"

"Oh, Bill, just shut up, will you?" She turned back to the dishes.

"All right, all right, you're a very big star. I should have known better."

"Just let me read for it." She kept her back to him, put the last fork in the drying rack. Silence. She switched off the overhead lamp, and headed into the living room. She wanted the part, and he wanted to sleep with her. It was sort of funny, she supposed. After all these years, after two marriages and two divorces, she had finally managed to make it to Bill's casting couch.

On the strength of Bill's support, the New York producers gave Carol the part of Mary L. Bill's unmarried sister, Cosette, would come to stay with the kids. *Raishtag*—Armenian for angel—was how she had greeted Aram each morning years ago when he was a baby and they were staying in the San Francisco house Bill had bought for his mother. Carol would come upstairs each morning from Bill's studio apartment holding Aram in her arms, and Cosette would be thrilled to see him. "*Raishtag . . . raishtag . . .* Good *morning, raishtag,*" she would coo at him. Then, finally, she would notice Carol.

"Mmm-hmm," she would mutter, looking away.

But that was years ago now. Cosette's life had been controlled by her mother Takoohi, who had turned her into her lifelong handmaiden. And after Takoohi died in 1950, Bill had more or less picked up with Cosette where their mother left off. So she was less infuriating to Carol than she had been—sadder, older. And she seemed to love Aram and Lucy.

Carol called Gloria to let her know she was coming and Gloria called back the next day to say she wanted her to stay in her studio on East Sixty-fourth Street between Madison and Fifth. Suddenly the papers were running stories about Gloria splitting with Leopold and taking their two sons, Stan and Chris, to live in a suite at the Ambassador Hotel with an around-the-clock bodyguard, apparently to

97

deter a confrontation with Stokowski. And she was supposed
to be dating Frank Sinatra. But Gloria wouldn't say anything, only telling her that she would pick her up at the
airport. It was the old story of Gloria's being private—but
Frank Sinatra, my God.

2

DURING HER THIRD WEEK IN NEW YORK, ONE SUNDAY
afternoon late in January, on an impulse, Carol waited for the
downtown Fifth Avenue bus in front of the Metropolitan Mu-
seum of Art. Fifth Avenue was darkening and yet the sky was
still a luminous, almost translucent blue. The gutters were
edged with old snow and the pavement, still wet, reflected
the headlights the cabs had started to turn on.

Carol knew an almost wild elation, dropping her nickel and
dime into the change machine on the half-filled bus, and taking
a window seat on the Central Park side as they headed downtown. It was a trip she knew from her childhood, those afternoons after school when she took the bus down to the Central
Park stables for riding lessons. It had all gotten to her then,
but without her quite knowing it. Suddenly, looking up over
Central Park into the lingering blue, she saw the lit neon sign
for the Essex House in the distance, just above the stripped
calligraphic black of the trees. There was such a heartbreaking
quality in the mix of New York day and night that moment.

Gloria had met her at the airport with Frank Sinatra, and had
taken her to the studio apartment, a wonderful, skylighted
room on the top floor of a four-story brownstone, filled with
flowers and candies Gloria and Frank had ordered, and three

of Gloria's own brightly colored paintings: a bouquet, a summer landscape, and a portrait of a woman who seemed a sort of cross between Gloria and Carol herself. It was like a dream, a marvelous room of her own.

Sinatra was terribly sweet and gallant, so unlike the bar brawler image he had, yet at the same time with that voice that effortlessly evoked the whole world of Saturday night. Gloria seemed radiantly happy. But only a few weeks later, Sinatra was gone and Gloria announced she was in love with Sidney Lumet, a young director just breaking into films from television, who had something of the look of the young Orson Welles. And not long after that, Carol attended their marriage ceremony, a very private one at the New York apartment of the playwright Sidney Kingsley and his wife, the actress Madge Evans. She marveled at the speed of Gloria's life, but her friend had never seemed more sure-footed. Carol even felt a small pang of envy, seeing how optimistically Gloria was beginning again.

Bill was at rehearsals for the play, of course, and took a kind of proprietary interest in her performance—to the point of volunteering to coach her on the part in the evenings at her studio. Naturally, the coaching led directly into sleeping with her, but of course she had known that it would.

The big news was that Gloria, too, was going to be in the play. She was going to play Elsie Mandelspiegel. The director, Sandy Meisner, had chosen her from his acting class for the role. Now Carol, too, began taking Sandy's classes—to help her get her feet again as an actress.

Carol really had only a single scene in the play, but it was a real scene, something that could go as far as she was ready to take it. It was a quiet moment in the jazzlike dance of the play, a dialogue between her and Joe, the barroom philosopher, who was played by Franchot Tone. "Is it Madge Lowry?" he asks her, referring to the initials M. L. on her suitcase. And he plays the guessing game into a subtle, finely paced little modern minuet between the two of them, complete with a couple of romantic floor-swooping turns. It was as if the scene had been written inside out, so that what was spoken was only the shadow of the real meaning, which was in the silences.

The audience was incredible. On the evening of the second preview she could feel it, almost as though it were a third person. She knew exactly when it was listening—knew just how long she could stretch each moment before she would lose it. She only let that happen once, although there was another, later moment that she shortened, slightly panicky because she had fumbled the earlier one.

Opening night, however, it worked straight through. She and Franchot Tone seemed to become the scene, so that they literally couldn't go wrong. The importance of the evening, she supposed, had brought everybody to their cutting edge.

The play opened to good notices, and her days now turned upside down. She had to be at the theater at seven-thirty each evening, instead of ten o'clock each morning, and it was usually after two in the morning by the time she'd unwound from the performance and could fall asleep. Then it would be noon before she was up and dressed.

After the play opened, Bill returned to California and she was really on her own for the first time in years—really for the first time *ever*, in a way. Jim Agee was in town and had taken the pages of her writing, which he still insisted would make a book, a novel, to his friend David MacDowell, an editor at Random House. Jim seemed very enthusiastic and hopeful about her chances.

When the six-week limited run of *The Time of Your Life* had almost ended, she got a call from David MacDowell, inviting her to lunch. He took her to the Colony, and told her right away that Random House wanted to publish the book. He was a man around Jim's age, which was also Bill's age, but of the old school: a Southern gentleman. She knew he was one of the great editors. There were a few things, of course, that he wanted her to work on, but they all felt it was a fine first novel.

That evening, sitting at the glass-topped table in the studio, she called the kids to tell them the news, on balance maybe the most important, meaningful news of her life. She was thirty years old, and Random House was going to publish her book.

After she told Aram and Lucy, Bill came on.

"What's the news, kid?"

"Bill, I'm so excited. Random House is going to publish my book."

"What book might that be?"

"You know, the book—the writing—I've been working on. I told you about it."

"There is no book, and I want to know when you will allow yourself to *be* yourself, instead of a congenital liar."

"Bill, I'm getting a contract. They're going to pay me."

"What're they paying you, kid?"

"Fifteen hundred dollars."

"You're a liar. But you go ahead and *be* a liar. Let's suppose that's what you *should* be right now. Is that the idea?"

"Bill, I can't really lie about it. Either they're going to publish it or not. They accepted it today."

"There is no book, kid, but that's all right. You go ahead and say that there is one. There may be some healing in that for you, and if there is, I'm for it."

Bill's certainty, she realized lying in the dark, barely visible studio room in the middle of the night, was almost enough to convince *her*. Maybe he was right. Maybe they weren't going to publish it. After all, David MacDowell had just rather casually told her they were going to, and that she was going to get a fifteen-hundred-dollar advance. But he hadn't *insisted* on it, the way Bill insisted they *weren't* going to publish it.

It was this very powerful idea he had of her that had ruined his life and had ruined her life, and would maybe ruin Aram's and Lucy's lives too. But there he was, inside it, eating and sleeping and typing and walking and all the other things in the world he did, including sleeping with her, and it somehow all went into this idea he had of what she was.

The idea was that she was nobody, nothing. A cipher. Zero. A bubble-gum wrapper on the sidewalk, blown into the gutter and sailing down the gutter water into the sewer, never to be seen again. She would never be known by anyone in the world except him and the few friends she had, who obviously had regarded her as a human being only out of some unaccountable aberration of their own. He *knew* she was useless, and he was angry—literally in a rage—if anyone believed that she had any value of any kind. It was all right, she supposed, if he himself, out of the crazy generosity of his heart, gave her a place in the larger scheme of things he commanded. The role in *The Time of Your Life*, say. But God forbid anyone else should decide to be generous to her—or worse yet, decide she had some genuine merit as an actress, a writer, or a woman.

He wanted her dead, she suddenly knew with that wide-awake clarity of early morning dark. It had to do with something in him, something that made him want to hate and punish her all the way to extinction. "Couldn't you just drive off a cliff, kid," he had asked her—with a half smile that sickened her more, if possible, than the words themselves—one day during the period of their second divorce. Why had she married him again? Because of the kids? *No* answer would really work, because it was just a dumb, really ghastly mistake. And his attitude really had nothing to do with her being this or that or all the ugly things he could call her and had called her.

It went way, way beyond any specific shortcoming of her own. She knew she had these, just as anyone had. She could be lazy. She could be silly. She could be superficial, and bitchy, or even manic and mean. She had been all of those things and more and worse. But that really had very little to do with it. Because Bill hardly noticed, one way or the other.

All it had to do with was his mood. Just his mood. If he was in a good mood and she was running around naked, screaming with her hair on fire, he would be pleased and comforted by her presence. If he was in a bad mood and she was in the best way she could possibly be on every score, he would be irritated by something about her, and make that an excuse to explode into rage.

The day before she left to go back to the Palisades, Gloria and Sidney gave her a big party at her apartment on Gracie Square to celebrate the book's acceptance.

The party was full of celebrities—Marilyn Monroe, so sweet-looking in a big yellow cardigan sweater and no makeup, sitting on the floor talking with Paula Strasberg, who sat in a chair beside her. Sammy Davis, Jr., arrived, laughing and punching Sidney on the arm. Then, she caught sight of Jim Agee standing by the piano near the windows in the living room. It was a white overcast day, but it was quite warm— it was early May now—and the big white-shuttered windows were open. The party, at least insofar as it was for her, was really about what *he* had done with her book, and she suddenly felt a rush of gratitude.

"Jim," she called across the room but he didn't hear. He was standing with a drink in his hand, talking with Sandy Meisner.

By this time, she was already in a kind of sprint across the room to him, and she didn't realize until she had all but reached him that he still hadn't seen her, and so hadn't moved to make room for her. And she couldn't quite stop short.

"Jim!" she said again, just before bumping and sort of bouncing off him. It was an awkward, strange moment. He turned to her, bewildered, and then broke into a grin.

"Hello, Carol."

Up close, his whole presence seemed to have a different texture than she remembered—somehow a rubbery consistency now. As always, he was extraordinary, so sweet to her, so full of congratulations. She was planning to dedicate the

103

book to him but she wanted it to be a surprise and didn't mention it.

She was back in the Palisades by the time she got the news of his death. He had had a heart attack in a New York taxicab the day after Gloria's party. Almost immediately, he began to be heralded as a major literary figure who had never gotten the acclaim he deserved. And it finally began to seem presumptuous of her to dedicate the book to him. It was her little first novel, and it would have been fine if he were alive, but once he died it was too easy to see it as a cheap self-promotion on her part, instead of the gesture she meant it to be.

3

THERE WAS ANOTHER LITTLE PILE OF LETTERS FROM KEN waiting for her when she got home. At first she thought she might pass up reading them altogether now, but one night after the kids had gone to bed, she had a little half-hour of fun with them, sitting Indian-style on her bed in her pink nightgown. "My radiant California sweetheart," he called her this time, among a lot of other nice things.

An agent she had signed with in New York, Jane Deacy, called in June, just after the kids had gotten out of school for the summer, to tell her that they wanted her to read for the new George Axelrod play, *Will Success Spoil Rock Hunter?*, which would be opening on Broadway in the fall. In the meantime, she had gone to the beauty parlor and had her hair done so she was a blonde again. Jane wasn't bothered by that at all, though, and even seemed to feel it might be better for her at the reading. She arranged to have Aram and Lucy stay with Jean and Dick Widmark in Mandeville Canyon for the two nights she'd be in New York.

She read for both of the female roles in the play—the sex-bomb movie queen who is the star, and the supporting role of the secretary. George Axelrod apparently wanted her for the lead, but Jules Stein, the producer, felt they needed someone more obvious for it, and Jayne Mansfield eventually got the part. She got word before she left for California that she had been cast as the secretary and would understudy for Mansfield. Rehearsals would be starting in August. She flew back on the Red Eye to Los Angeles, knowing that this was it—the end of a line, the beginning of a new one. She was going to move back to New York. Life was going to start over again for her. F. Scott Fitzgerald might even have been wrong about American lives not having second acts. Maybe he *was* wrong about that.

Aram and Lucy weren't thrilled. Aram was in Little League, and Lucy had gotten to be friends with a nine-year-old girl named Debbie who lived around the corner on Las Pulgas. But Carol sat them both down at the dining room table one night and told them how important the move might be, not just for her life but for their lives, too, and although she wasn't absolutely positive they understood what she was getting at— she mentioned the museums, the theaters and art galleries, the broader horizons of life there—or even if she herself understood it (New York was like light to her, even at night, while the Palisades, paradoxically, with all its sunshine, seemed to exist in ceaseless dark), both of them were terribly sweet.

"I wasn't sure before, Mom," Aram, who was now eleven, said, "but now that you told me about it, I *want* to go."

Bill, on the other hand, had another idea. His *one* idea. He wanted her to stay in the Palisades and die. He tried to make her come to her senses, as he put it.

"If you go," he told her, "not one more penny. That's it, kid. Not one cent again. I mean it."

"But Bill, you know the money's not for me. It's for Aram and Lucy."

"You figure it any way you like, kid. But not one more red, stinking cent—ever."

She had refused both alimony and community property in her divorce settlement. Bill's idea of her as a fortune huntress was too much of a comfort to his ego for her to provide supporting evidence of any kind. It was laughable, anyway, because the big upheavals during their first marriage had to do with his discovery of her early background, which she had been frightened enough to hide from him before they were married. Perhaps she had known even then, if not on a conscious level, that as the son of immigrant Armenians he wanted to marry a real Park Avenue heiress, which he had apparently assumed her to be and she was perhaps all too willing to allow him to believe. And yet the idea was that *she* was the social climber. It was too absurd, too much of an insane self-deception on his part, for her not to relish telling her lawyer, Jerry Geisler, not to ask for anything but child support. Geisler had even told her that he felt she was making a serious error—not so much for herself, perhaps, as for her children—and begged her to reconsider on their behalf.

But there was another motive, beneath this one, that Carol kept unspoken. And yet it was this one that had probably been decisive. She knew too many women who had become alimony queens. They took their ex-husbands to the cleaner's in court, and forever after lived in a sort of sober, resentful splendor—really too well taken care of ever to need to venture out their front doors again. And any man who paid a call was in immediate competition with the alimony portfolio. Their security, in effect, became a trap that stunted any real future they might have made for themselves, though none of the women Carol knew seemed to be even remotely aware of it. Rather, they had developed terribly fussy temperaments and become more and more rigid in their own daily patterns, so that the only sort of man who might squeeze himself into their lives would be one who would somehow find it possible to take the shape of a combination butler and gigolo. She knew one Hollywood divorcée, still in her thirties, who didn't at all mind sleeping with her various suitors—and there were a few—but who would not allow any of them to spend the night in her Beverly Hills home. Her attitude was, "You can fuck me, but don't you dare bring your toothbrush or shaving kit." She imagined she had everything: sex when she liked, but no one messing up her bathroom. Knowing some of these women before their divorces, Carol saw them as the fatal bargain hunters of life—the ones who get such a good deal they don't realize they've bought a hideous existence as part of the package. And it never dawned on them somehow. Even her mother, who had been separated from Daddy for several years now, was in this danger, although moving to Rome, as she wanted to do, might be what she needed. There was a possibility that Carol would stay in her new apartment at 970 Park Avenue when she first arrived with the kids.

"Of course you can!" her mother had shouted on the phone. "Haven't I always done whatever I could for you, Carol? Haven't I?"

"Of course, Mother."

"You don't even have to pay rent."

That meant that she *did* have to pay, as of course she had planned to do. She would feel uneasy, she knew, living there—but her mother would be leaving for Rome very soon after they arrived. It was only three or four rooms, which she knew would be hard on the kids after the Palisades, but that was all they really needed. And they would be right around the corner from P.S. 6, which was supposed to be the best public school in Manhattan.

4

I⊤ WAS A VERY HOT, MUGGY THURSDAY AFTERNOON LATE
in July in 1955 when they got off the plane. Daddy picked
her up at the airport and they were taken in his chauffeur-
driven, air-conditioned Cadillac to "Grandma's," as he had
always called her mother, even before Aram and Lucy were
born (because he himself was old enough to be Carol's grandfather?). It was always such a reassurance to see Daddy: he
was, she supposed, one of the very few truly civilized men
she had ever known. "Let me know, darlin', how I can help,"
he told her as she got out of the car at Eighty-third Street and
Park.

The heat, she knew, was going to be an initial shock for
the kids. Aram's and Lucy's faces had flushed a high pink
almost the moment they got off the plane. The sight of their
faces had put her heart in her throat. What if she was making
a big, fat mistake, after all?

The first thing they told her at the *Rock Hunter* rehearsals was
that they wanted her to lose ten to fifteen pounds for the role.
Not that she was fat, but at five feet three she couldn't afford
an extra pound as an ingenue and the understudy for the lead.
She had only six weeks before the first out-of-town opening
in Philadelphia. She got a Dexamyl prescription from an old
beau of Elinor's, who now had a general practice on Madison
Avenue around the corner from her mother's. She took one
pill with coffee each morning, and it was then very easy not
to have lunch at all, and to pick up just a hamburger for dinner.

Her weight began to drop almost immediately.

At the same time, the pills gave her more energy than she'd ever had before. Suddenly she looked forward to the mornings—a time when she had always felt as though the whole world knew some secret she hadn't been told. The doctor had mentioned to her that her blood pressure was a little on the low side, so maybe that was the reason. She didn't really get going until after dark. But now, a half hour after she had taken the pill, the morning would open up to her, as rich and exhilarating as any midnight.

She would get up with the kids, and once the governess she hired for them—a middle-aged Scottish woman named Janet Law—arrived at eight-thirty, she would be virtually bursting to get out onto Madison Avenue for a morning walk before reporting to rehearsals at ten. It was too early for the real heat of the day, and she relished seeing the city just beginning to go into gear: the shopkeepers opening their doors, some of them watering down the pavement in front of their stores. She window-shopped, and made a habit of stopping at a magazine store in the seventies to pick up the morning *Times*. She imagined she would read the paper during an idle stretch at rehearsals, but after glancing at the headlines— Stevenson had just announced he would run against Eisenhower again in 1956; Senator Estes Kefauver's subcommittee on juvenile delinquency was investigating the effects of comic books—and turning to the theater news during the first available lull, she would seldom read further, although there was plenty of time for it. She was too keyed up with the excitement of seeing the play take shape day by day. It was a wonderful cast, a real gang of people who all enjoyed one another. Even Jayne Mansfield, who had the biggest boobies in the world and had them hanging out in every magazine in town, was just a sweet, simple girl who loved the idea of being a big star and having all the men in the world gaga over her.

• • •

After the rehearsals let out, between five and six, Carol often shared a cab home with Walter Matthau, a young actor who played the writer in the play, and who lived farther uptown. "I'll drop you off," he had suggested one evening, and henceforth this became a routine. For some reason, he absolutely refused to let her pay for any part of the fare. "I'm going anyway," he'd say to her with charming exasperation. "Will you put your money away!" He was a tall, rangy man in his middle thirties who had a wonderful quality in the play, a kind of quiet intelligence that brought the writer vividly to life. He was somewhat quiet sometimes during their cab rides together, and she was a little uneasy with silence in people, but whenever she said anything she was reassured by the casual warmth of his reply. He was one of those men she found more attractive and interesting each time she saw him. Naturally, he was married.

One night in early November, after the tryouts were over and they had opened to good reviews in New York, out of the blue he told Carol his wife was out of town and asked if she'd like to go to a Knicks-Celtics game with him since he had two tickets. She wasn't terribly excited by the prospect of a basketball game, but the casual ease she had begun to feel in his presence made being with him fun. She said yes. The basketball game turned out to be very colorful, they had hot dogs and Cokes, and Walter reacted so strongly to certain moments in the game that she wasn't surprised when he told her he had a small bet on the Knicks.

It was an actor in the cast of *Rock Hunter* who made a casual reference to Walter's apartment, "around the corner," meaning, she found out, around the corner from the theater. Suddenly she realized that all those nights he was "dropping her off" in the taxi, it wasn't on his way at all. He had been doing it to spend time with her. By now, in any case, she had sensed that there was more to his seeing her than casual friendliness.

• • •

Ken Tynan dashed into town and took her out to lunch. She took him, in turn, to a couple of parties at Gloria's on Gracie Square. He still wanted to marry her. Couldn't she come to Europe? No, she couldn't. He had been in Egypt, where William Faulkner had been drinking so much he seemed to have a permanent case of the shakes. "I've got to shake this cold," he told Ken, and Ken, in turn, repeated it everywhere. He was a sort of connoisseur—of everything.

When he went back to Europe, the letters came again, now to her New York address. They continued all the pledges of his undying devotion. He was there, somehow steadfastly, in the back of her life, dependably clamoring for something that had more to do with an idea in his mind than with her the way she actually was. It was so unremittingly intense, and yet nothing was really going on, was it?

After staying four months, she found someone to sublet her mother's apartment to, and she took a lease on the third floor apartment at 53 East Ninety-third Street, the house that had been the one used in the old spy movie *The House on 92nd Street*. Directly across the street was a huge, old building, a former embassy, that Billy Rose had remodeled and turned into his home. Her new apartment was quite small: in the front, a living room that also would serve as her bedroom; along a corridor, a kitchenette and a bathroom; and in the back, two small bedrooms, one for Aram and one for Lucy. But it was much cheaper than her mother's place, which was predictably depressing for her in any case. She delighted now in finding little not-too-expensive pieces of furniture, or fabric, or whatnots that struck her as right for the apartment, the first of her life on her own.

Gloria came over one night and they ended up spying on Billy Rose, who was walking through the lighted rooms of his palatial dwelling across the street. He was wearing a fitted white shirt and dark gray slacks with black suspenders. He moved an art deco lamp across a table, trying different angles. They both knew him slightly—less as a Broadway legend than a fellow party-goer.

"Billy's like 'the little king,' isn't he?" Carol said at the window. They had turned off the living room lights so they would be less obvious if he looked up and out.

Then, still watching him, they made a plan. Gloria would disguise herself and knock on Billy's door, soliciting for charity.

"Let's give Billy's wealth a real test, shall we, darling?" Gloria said in a conspiratorial whisper.

"Oh yes," Carol answered, smiling in the dark, "but as we know, that's always a very dangerous thing to do."

They turned on the living room lights again and found a large, dark scarf of Carol's and an old raincoat of Bill's that was somehow in Carol's closet. By the time Gloria went downstairs, the scarf hiding half her face, the raincoat a roomy, lopsided fit, she was unrecognizable. Carol closed the front door, turned off the lights again and went back to the window.

Gloria crossed the street under the street lights and approached the entrance of Billy's mansion with a slightly hunchbacked aspect and appeared to ring the doorbell so many times that Billy's concentration, now applied to the position of the chaise longue in the second floor parlor, was irremediably disturbed. Carol spied him, with an uncertain look on his face, leaving the chair in midmaneuver and disappearing from the room.

A moment or two later, the front door opened and Gloria—using full theatrical projection so that Carol could hear her across the street and in a voice that sounded as if it came out of a cracked accordion—said to Billy, "I'm soliciting donations for the Czechoslovakian refugees!"

A diminutive but powerfully assertive Napoleonesque figure, Billy stage-boomed back at her: "I'm a very busy man and you just disturbed me while I was working. Don't you ever ring my doorbell again!"

He was about to slam the door when Gloria went into a fast pirouette, virtually unwinding out of her costume.

"Billy, it's me!" she shrieked. "It's Gloria!"

"Gloria!" Billy boomed again, still obviously bewildered. "Well, for crying out loud. Come on in!"

Gloria waved up at Carol and Carol waved back at her and then Billy waved, too. He invited them both over for a drink. He was still slightly uneasy, but gracious. They sat in the room with the chaise longue still in its design limbo. There was an original Renoir of a French servant girl on the wall beside them.

Seeing Gloria look at the Renoir, Carol was reminded of how much her friend loved to paint—a throwback to her Aunt Gertrude? Gloria had new paintings on the walls almost every time she visited her at Gracie Square. She seemed to be working steadily. Carol loved the colors she used.

A few weeks later, Gloria had a huge package delivered to Carol's apartment. It turned out to be an enormous portrait of Carol she had painted from memory, and it had to be one of Gloria's very best paintings, a sort of cross between a Milton Avery and a Marie Laurencin. Carol was seen seated, three-quarter length, and gazing directly out from the painting. There was something luminous and semitransparent about her presence. The colors were pastel pink, orange and green— and two dark brown, very round, eyes. (Carol's eyes were, in fact, green, but often looked brown because of her large pupils.) She put the painting up over the foldout convertible couch she used as her bed in the living room. It gave the room a lovely center of color, a kind of delicate hearth.

A few years before, Gloria had sent a framed Avedon photograph of herself, signed with love, to Carol in the Palisades. She remembered how she and Bill and the kids had all joked about the megalomania of the gesture. Now, with the arrival of this marvelous painting, Carol felt more than a twinge of guilt. It was so simple, really: Gloria sent her the photograph of herself because she loved her; and that was the same reason she painted the portrait of Carol and sent it. That was just the way she was.

Just after her book, *The Secret in the Daisy*, was published to good reviews, Truman Capote, whom she had gradually gotten to know better over the years, invited Carol for a Sunday night dinner at his brownstone in Brooklyn Heights. She had expected at least a small gathering, but when she arrived she discovered she was the only guest. He had cooked a Southern Creole chicken recipe by himself and made a beautiful candlelit table for the two of them. He told her he liked her book.

"You've got a mind like a lime crystal, honey," he drawled out sweetly over after-dinner wine.

Later in the evening, sitting on his sofa in an oversize yellow cardigan sweater, the same style sweater Marilyn Monroe had worn at Gloria's, he read to her from *Breakfast at Tiffany's*, which he had nearly finished. He had been rewriting the last sentence over and over again for weeks, and had just gotten it. Before they said goodbye that night, he said he wanted her to know that the head of one of the television networks, one of the most powerful men in America, was a big fan of hers and had asked Truman if he could introduce him to her.

"But he's married, of course," Carol said.

"Oh yes," Truman answered, "but he'd take good care of you, honey, that's one thing you wouldn't have to worry about."

"No thanks," Carol said blithely, picking up a little of Holly Golightly's insouciance. "That's all Bill would need to take Aram and Lucy away from me."

"A lot of people would say you're crazy, honey," Truman said, looking almost like a little boy curled up in his big sweater in the lamplight, "but I think you're just the sweetest little thing in this whole damn city, I do."

Late that fall, Walter Matthau rented a one-room sixth floor apartment on Central Park West, overlooking the park. His second child, a daughter, had been born, but the marriage was obviously in trouble. He was one of the most respected New York actors, one who had made his reputation on Broadway with rave reviews in a series of commercial flops, but she knew he had very little money. Why was he renting his own studio? It suddenly occurred to Carol that one of the things she had never allowed herself—or maybe had never had time for—was a simple, "no regrets" affair. Everything had always been so momentously serious for her. She had probably missed out on the fun everybody else was having taking things lightly.

All Walter had in his room was a double bed and an enormous antique bureau with a hundred little drawers, mostly empty. The one she seemed invariably to open contained only an old wristwatch. Their affair started one night in his apartment in as natural a way as, a little while later, a thunderstorm began. She lay in bed, breathing the strange, lacquered fragrance of the "new" apartment, watching the lightning blanch the window and listening to the thunder that afterwards erupted from various parts of the sky. The quality and duration of the noise was absolutely unpredictable, and yet at the same time utterly inevitable each time—like some extraordinary piece of music. Walter had fallen asleep beside her. On an impulse, she got up and tiptoed naked to the windows. They had no curtains and Walter liked to keep the blinds up. There was a flash now that illuminated the buildings along Central Park South and the part of Central Park that lay in front of her. Carol waited. Then, with a slow, majestic certainty the thunder broke in a long, complicated arpeggio. It was thrilling: she felt alive inside much larger life.

After a run of nearly a year and a half, the play closed during the winter of 1957, and Carol fell back on her unemployment checks and began looking for another job. Walter went to the West Coast for several weeks to do the movie *King Creole* with Elvis Presley. Their affair had begun so casually that at first it escaped her that the edginess she felt after a few days of his absence had to do with her missing him. When it occurred to her that this was what it was about, she didn't know whether to feel better or worse. Now she was involved with a married man and maybe she was kidding herself that she could take it lightly. Walter called every few days and told her funny stories about the job. He had to break a balsa wood chair over Elvis's head in a fight scene. When they shot the scene, Elvis was in some kind of pain. It turned out that a boil on Elvis's head had broken when Walter brought the chair down on him during the fight.

"I miss you, Walter," she told him, broadly yet at the same time shyly.

"I miss you too, pussycat."

That spring, when he came back into town, they took long evening walks down Madison Avenue, stopping at a Calico Kitchen or Hamburger Heaven to have hamburgers or just coffee. They couldn't really sleep together in the apartment at Ninety-third Street because she never knew just when Lucy or Aram would be up to use the bathroom. Janet Law, the kids' governess, whom Daddy helped her pay for, shared Lucy's bedroom now. So they would walk to Walter's apartment and then, afterwards, walk around the south end of the park, past the Plaza Hotel with its line of horses and buggies, that landmark of her girlhood, and now late into the night, up Fifth or Madison.

In his own childhood, Walter had known a very different New York. He had grown up on the Lower East Side in a series of cold-water flats with his mother and his older brother. He told her the only room where he could get enough peace and quiet to do his homework was the bathroom. If he ever made a lot of money, he wanted to build a house that would have a bathroom so large he could have an office in it.

Their lovemaking was better than Carol had ever known.

Walter was really, when it came right down to it, just a guy who seemed to be crazy about her. Her sure sense of him in turn released her.

And then all of a sudden that summer, it came to her that she was in over her head. She thought she would just be casual, just have an affair with an ordinary guy; leave the geniuses, like Bill, for someone with more stomach for suffering; she'd had her fill. She and Walter had fun being together. That was what it was all about. Wherever they were, whatever they were doing, there was a current of pleasure that ran through it. Even if it was just going to see *From Here to Eternity* on Forty-second Street one night on an impulse. Or having hot dogs at an all-night Nedick's on Broadway afterwards. It was the growing certainty of her knowledge that he would never—with that irrational, animal ferocity she had seen again and again in Bill—turn on her. Rather, she felt Walter was someone more or less like her. He was difficult at times, petty or irritable, but it was never something really beyond her own reckoning. He told her his marriage had foundered a while ago, even before he met her—but at the same time she knew he wasn't the sort of man who would end a marriage easily. He was worried about his wife and children, uncertain about the future—things that were readily understandable to her.

But falling in love had never been part of her emotional agenda. The idea was something casually comfortable, and yet passion seemed to have grown out of that. Bill had taken Aram and Lucy to Europe for the summer. Meanwhile, Ken had been writing at least once a week that she must meet him in Spain for the bullfight season, that it was high time she let him show her his side of life. She wasn't about to fall for Ken Tynan—but even so, was he still married, or what? She had no idea.

She and Walter had an argument one night about his going to visit his mother for a Sunday dinner at her apartment on

West Thirty-sixth Street. Rose Matthau seemed to be a tough old lady. She had raised Walter and his brother, Henry, single-handedly after their father went off with another woman when Walter was ten. Carol thought his mother plumbed whole, deep reservoirs of guilt in her dutiful younger son unmercifully, and she sensed that Rose, whom for obvious reasons she hadn't met, wasn't terribly nice to Walter into the bargain. It was a stupid argument, really none of her business. She wanted to go to a Sunday night Actors' Benefit with Walter to see Julie Harris and Chris Plummer in *The Lark*, and she was just being selfish about it.

Alone that night in the Ninety-third Street apartment—Walter had gone to see Rose in the end; in certain ways he could be very stubborn—it occurred to her that going to see Ken Tynan was maybe the way out of a situation that was turning out to be deeper and more demanding than she had ever had in mind. In any case, Walter would be going to the West Coast again for a month or so of television jobs. This would give her a chance to get away, too, to let the relationship relax out of an ardor that had first surprised and then upset her. Maybe the way to keep it casual was to simply see someone else for a while.

She told Walter she would be going to see Oona, which of course she hoped to do. They hadn't talked in so long; she had moments of keenly missing her dearest friend. And it turned out that Carol left for Madrid and Walter left for Hollywood within twenty-four hours of each other.

5

SHE ARRIVED IN MADRID IN A HAZY, BROWNISH NOON, and saw Ken, a towering figure among the neat, dark Spaniards, standing in a white linen suit observing her with a wry smile from the other side of customs. When they had checked her through, he hugged her warmly, and kissed her on both cheeks.

"Saroyan, you are ravishing. We're going to lunch at Horcher's. I'm afraid we've just got time to drop off your bags at the hotel."

She waited in the taxi while Ken took her bags in at the Hotel Ritz. The restaurant was very fancy—he told her it was one of the best in Europe—and she let him order for them both. This he did with great relish and flair, in a Spanish accent that could only belong to an English aristocrat. Then, after this flamboyant performance, which had drawn baffled looks from surrounding tables, he turned to her very warmly, eyes twinkling.

"Well, so you finally came. I'm so glad. Now you will find out who I am."

"But only in separate rooms, right?"

"As I said in my letters, *and* on the phone, that's fine with me."

"Good."

"But you *will* marry me, Saroyan. You know that you will. And, furthermore, I can *see* that you know it."

She smiled and said she knew she couldn't marry anyone because she was such a terrible wife any man would go mad. Ken laughed and said that's what he loved about her, that she was solely and completely a woman to adore. The house-keeping would have to be taken care of by someone else, although he knew she was lying about that because he had seen her in her immaculate California house.

They had a fine, delicate paella. And breaking her routine, Carol drank two glasses of sangria, which made her quite drunk. After lunch, they took a walk through an elegant, well-kept park surrounded by the downtown buildings. There was a slight, very welcome breeze now.

"Can you feel it?" Ken asked her.

"What?"

"The fact that we are walking around in the middle of a totalitarian state."

"I don't know."

"I don't know if I can either. Maybe it's just the Spanish temperament, which is high tragedy, as you'll see tomorrow at the bullfight. And we must go to the Prado to see the Bosch paintings. Do you want a drink?"

"No, I'm already a little tipsy."

"I know. I meant water." He gestured to a small, ordinary-looking water fountain under a beautiful, languishing willow tree.

"Oh, I'm sorry. No thanks. My God, it's like a little piece of Paterson, New Jersey, in the middle of Madrid."

He took her arm and guided her to the paved path at the right. They passed three dark men wearing fezzes.

"Oh, that reminds me of Bill," she said.

Ken laughed. "He doesn't wear one, does he?"

"No, no, never. But he meets people like that and they step into tiny rooms and one stands up and makes a speech honoring him. Bill gets very bored, but he never stops going with them."

"Armenians?"

"I don't know. I know they're not Jews."

• • •

Their rooms were next to each other, but did not adjoin, and she was very glad to have a sanctuary after an early light supper at the hotel.

"I'll let you catch your breath now," Ken told her, leaving her at the door at around seven with a light kiss on the forehead.

The room overlooked a huge circle—a park with statuary—around which the traffic ran. They were on the sixth floor. The room seemed fairly ordinary, no obvious frills, other than a full bath, which she supposed might be a luxury in Spain.

She bathed, got into a nightgown and robe, and reviewed her six dresses, which she had hung up that afternoon. She planned to wear them in a succession that would build up to the best one: a two-hundred-dollar black and red Chanel that was all she had managed to get out of her first marriage to Bill. That and—not to forget—her life.

She noticed a few pieces of American change she had brought with her on the bureau. A quarter, three pennies, and a nickel—so serious, small, and odd-looking, suddenly, next to the huge, negotiable pesetas. Maybe it was just that you never really looked at money until you were somewhere you couldn't spend it.

She got into bed as the sky was going dark and the lights began twinkling below. It was a strange sensation having so much uninterrupted space outside, no windows opposite her window, but volumes of night air out there, and then, all the way across the park, lit windows like her own, but tiny in the distance.

Ken had left a copy of his book, *Persona Grata*, made up of his theater reviews, on her bed table, and now, sitting up in bed, she began to read it. He was quite wonderful as a critic, very sort of dashing, and yet so far as she could tell, fair-minded too. He could get bitchy, of course, but then that's what critics were all about, she supposed, except for one or two very special ones. Brooks Atkinson in *The New York Times* wasn't the *writer* Ken was, and yet he was remarkable for the generosity with which he approached each play, trying to point to at least *something* that had been good about even the most dismal failure.

She wondered what it would be like to be reviewed by Ken. She saw the head of the fish she had seen at Horcher's that afternoon, the dead glazed eye surrounded by colorful garnishes, wheeled around on a cart. She had put the book down and she didn't want to forget to turn out the lamp on the bed table. But she had already done this and begun to dream.

6

THE BULLFIGHT TURNED OUT TO BE MORE INTERESTING than she expected. It was a hot afternoon, and they had good close seats. Ken coached her on some of the high drama and expertise of the ritual. At first, her favorite part was the *banderilleros:* two men who appeared near the beginning of each fight, wearing tight, sequined costumes, and who would run at and stick the bull in his neck with two long, brightly decorated darts that stayed in the bull from then on and kept reminding her of the toothpicks with colored cellophane ruffles stuck in steaks or sandwiches at restaurants.

Then, at the end of the third fight, one of the bullfighters did something very brave and beautiful, working with the small red cloth very close to where they sat. She could see the beads of sweat on his forehead as he concentrated on the huge, black, unpredictable form in front of him.

It was as if he were concentrating on a blind muscle of nature that had the power to kill him, but if his mind and body were finely tuned enough he could make it do what he wanted it to do. The young matador stood very erect and handsome and he moved very little and very slowly, bending slightly back and to the side, as the black cloud of the bull went for the small red cloth in a fury.

"*Olé!*" the crowd would roar after each long, graceful pass.

Then the bullfighter would move swiftly; she could hear a sort of nervous flutter of his feet to set up the cloth before the bull again without breaking the animal's spell of concentration. The bull's mind seemed to be held tautly intent by the bullfighter as he executed a dozen or more passes, until, at the end of these, the bull was both mesmerized and exhausted.

Then the bullfighter brought the sword out, holding it straight out in front of him at the bull, and then putting it behind the top of the red cloth. The bull charged now at a single flick he gave to the red cloth. It was as if the bullfighter had somehow mastered the bull's character, and so had control of his destiny.

"The braver the bull," Ken whispered to her, "the better the fight."

When he brought the sword out now, there was a long moment in which the matador stood in front of the bull, no longer holding up the red cloth. The sun glinted off the white blade. Then, making the moment both swift and powerfully charged, as the bull's head hung before him, the bullfighter plunged the sword up to its hilt into the body of the bull, entering at the base of his neck. The animal made a sudden move toward him, the bullfighter stepped to the side, and, all four legs giving out under him, the bull collapsed onto the brown, dusty, blood-spilled turf.

The crowd was on its feet in a roar of approval. Ken told her it was a perfect kill.

Before catching the train for Seville the following afternoon, they visited the Prado to see the Bosch paintings. The canvases were large and minutely painted. In one corner a house would be burning down; in another part of the painting a man who had the head of a weasel would be chasing a girl. They stood on the cool, echoing stone floors of the Prado, looking.

"Bosch is magnificent," Ken said. "He's the night to Brueghel's day."

The paintings were dizzying to Carol—wild extravaganzas of hell. Every so often she felt a sudden, fugitive flicker of wonder at herself for being where she was. Ken had not, not yet, pressed very hard to sleep with her, but she could feel it coming and she wondered what she would do when it happened.

At the train station, she noticed a cigarette machine containing only European cigarette brands, the colors and designs all very different from the American brands. It was like a cigarette machine in a dream. Only it wasn't a dream; it was Spain and she was with Ken Tynan. She wondered what Walter was doing.

7

THEY STAYED AT A MUCH SMALLER HOTEL ON A LITTLE back street in Seville, where they were having a bullfight festival. After dinner, Ken walked back to her second-floor room with her, and then, at the last moment, said he wanted to speak with her and asked her to come to his room, which was next door. In his room—like her own, very simple and elegant with its white linen and dark brown wooden furniture—he offered her a brandy, which she declined, and then poured one for himself and turned to her. Putting his hands on her shoulders, he looked directly into her eyes.

"I am madly," he told her, "—madly, passionately and irredeemably in love with you. I love you. I love you. I love you. And I want you to *let* me love you."

The moment had arrived, Carol realized, instantly breathless. Somehow, she could no longer really fight it. Ken turned and went to turn off the lights—the room was suddenly in darkness. He came back to her and kissed her and took her hand, guiding her to sit down beside him on the bed. There, he took her in his arms and kissed her again, and then lay down and gently pulled her down beside him. Although she didn't resist, Carol felt uneasy. What was it, really, that Ken saw in her, she wondered, as he kissed her and kissed her again. She imagined he somehow saw her as a little girl.

All of a sudden, then, she had a chilling sensation. She could swear the door to Ken's room opened and someone came in. She stiffened, yet Ken, who was above her, kissing her, with his back to the door, took no heed. She looked out into the dimness of the room and she became certain she saw someone's outline standing just to one side at the end of the bed.

"Ken!" she gasped, her voice choked, her body instantaneously breaking into a cold sweat.

"Yes, my sweet girl," he answered, his voice thick, almost gravelly.

"Ken, there's someone in the room!" She could barely get the words out, barely breathe.

Now Ken stiffened, pushing himself up, turning.

And then, out of the darkness at the edge of the bed came a man's voice.

"I'm terribly, terribly sorry." It was an oddly pleasant, gentle voice, with just a trace of a brogue. "My name is Patrick O'Sullivan and I'm employed by Baxter and Boice law offices in London, who represent Mrs. Tynan. I'm very, very sorry."

Carol sat up now, crossing her arms in front of her, holding her shoulders, and addressed the figure, the barest outline of whose face and form began to take shape as her eyes became acclimated to the darkness. "You've seen what you came to see. Now will you please leave."

"I will," answered the figure, and it immediately began to recede. The door opened, making a sudden, bold essay of light into the room, and then closed, leaving the room dark again. He was gone. Ken was up now and turned on the light.

"My God!" he said, in a state of obvious, disheveled shock.

Carol had rearranged her dress, and now stood up from the bed, straightening it some more.

"I've got to go," she said. "I can't stay here. I can't see you again until your wife calls off her dogs."

"Of course," he answered, real pain in his look.

"My ex-husband is constantly looking to take the kids away from me and have me declared an unfit mother, and this is all he needs to hear about."

"Whatever you want to do. I'm so sorry."

8

THE NEXT MORNING SHE TOOK A BUS TO MADRID, AND then caught a plane to Nice, where the Chaplins, usually at Vevey, were on a summer holiday. Oona picked her up at the airport that afternoon. There was a kind of still luminescence here—everything looked slightly translucent, so different from the heavy, darker colors of Spain. Oona and Charlie had rented a villa for the summer. When the chauffeur-driven Cadillac pulled up to the rose-arbored front entrance, Charlie came out the front door to greet them. At sixty-eight, he looked magnificently healthy and robust, with his white hair, white bushy eyebrows, and perennially pink cheeks. He was wearing white pants, a white crew-neck sweater, and tennis shoes, and his step still had that spring in it.

Carol knew, of course, that Oona had found her life. In the

summer of 1952, the Chaplins had left America by boat for a vacation in Europe. They were informed after a few days at sea that Charlie would be subject to examination by American officials before he would be allowed to re-enter the country; this after he'd been put through a long wait but finally cleared for a re-entry permit before they left. It was the McCarthy era, and Charlie was being hounded for his left-liberal associations, although he repeatedly insisted he was simply an artist—and as such a citizen of the world—whose sympathies would always be more complex than any flag or banner, right *or* left, could symbolize. But the Attorney General had actually declared that Charlie must "show proof of moral worth." After that, the Chaplins decided to take up permanent residence in Switzerland. Carol knew that Oona had even made a quick, secret airline trip back to America to get their money out of California because Charlie, of course, now couldn't do that.

Just before they left, Oona's father had been very ill, and she told Carol she'd written him at Doctors Hospital in New York, but hadn't come from California because she was pregnant with their fourth child. She had sent the letter along with photographs of the family in the care of Saxe Commins, her father's editor and closest friend, and he had given the big envelope to O'Neill in his hospital room but couldn't report to her whether or not he'd actually read the letter or looked at the photographs. By the time the family was in New York to take the ship to Europe, O'Neill was out of the hospital and in his wife Carlotta's care in Marblehead, Massachusetts.

During her father's final bedridden years, then, Oona wasn't able to see him, and she eventually—probably out of very justifiable anger, Carol supposed—took the step of renouncing her own American citizenship to become a British subject, like Charlie.

"Well," Charlie said, after giving Carol a warm hug, "how do you like the way your friend looks?" He turned to Oona, who was smiling radiantly at him behind her sunglasses. "Doesn't she look wonderful?"

"More beautiful, Charlie, than ever before," Carol answered, nodding with a kind of sweet solemnity from Oona to Charlie, as the chauffeur took her bags into the house.

"And you know," Charlie continued, smiling and now putting an arm around his wife, "I've made her a very rich woman. Yes, she's quite well off, you know."

"Oh, darling," Oona chided him with a grin, "really!"

"Oh yes," he went on, delightedly, "your friend is quite well fixed. Of course, she *has* embarrassed me with all these children, but other than that—"

"Charlie!" Oona kept smiling.

"Come in, come in," he said, laughing now; and putting an arm around each, he led them through the rose-trellised doorway.

The three of them had dinner that night on the second-floor terrace outside Oona and Charlie's bedroom. The four children had eaten earlier in the kitchen. Carol could hear their sweet voices below in the garden playing. Then she heard Kay-Kay, their nurse, calling the two younger daughters into bed.

"Vicky! Josie! Come now, it's nearly eight-thirty!"

Having heard that she had come from a visit with Ken Tynan, Charlie was rather paternally concerned, and even censorious. "My dear," he told her over a dessert of strawberries and crème fraîche, "the man is a theater critic. I mean you must try to be realistic. You must ask yourself the question: How much could a theater critic possibly earn in a year? I'm only thinking of your good. You know that."

"Oh, I know, Charlie," Carol answered. "Of course, you're right." How dear it was to have Charlie as a counselor; she had forgotten how much he loved the role. Then again, he had strongly counseled her against leaving Bill, so he wasn't necessarily an oracle.

Oona, who was standing behind him, having brought in a

dish of fruit from their bedroom, raised her eyebrows twice at Carol, smiling at Charlie's familiar assumption of the role of Dutch uncle.

Carol's room was directly over their bedroom. Oona took her up to say goodnight, and they ended up—as both knew they would—sitting up talking into the morning hours.

"Charlie's been awful this week," Oona told her, reclining in a big chair upholstered with a blue and white French provincial fabric. "Kay-Kay's getting on in years, you know."

"Of course," Carol answered, sitting up barefoot against the upholstered pillows on her bed.

"But, you know, it's been very hot lately. And the other morning she appeared in shorts, before taking the kids down to the beach. Well, he's been going out of his mind."

"Kay-Kay's legs aren't the best?"

Oona giggled. "Well, darling, you know, she's in her fifties. But he has no sympathy for her, which you would think he might. I was really surprised, because he's usually so understanding. He just told me to get her to wear long pants or a dress—that it put him off his food."

Both of them laughed a long time.

When she began to recover, Oona added, "And of course, I've just been going crazy, really crazy, trying to figure out *how* to tell her. I mean, what do you say?"

"Oh," Carol answered in the slightly clipped voice with which she signaled her comic turn, "that's my *favorite* problem. You and Gloria have the *best* problems. Because my other favorite is whether a man loves me for my money. Imagine having those things to worry about."

"How is she, anyway," Oona asked, smiling. "I mean is this Sidney nice?"

"Oh very, I think," Carol said, returning to her mainstream tone. "The main thing, of course, is she really adores him. I mean she's madly, madly in love. But..."

Oona narrowed her eyes at her. "But *what?*"

"Oh, I don't know. The really sweet thing about Gloria is that she's just a girl underneath everything. She's just like us. Of course. And she's crazy about Sidney. She really is. And I'm just not sure he trusts that. If he'd ask or just assume that of her, she would, I know, adore it. But I think maybe he's got this idea she's Gloria Vanderbilt, you know?"

"Which could really get in the way."

"That's her albatross. But she's so terribly sweet. The funny thing is, I think she may be the biggest romantic of the three of us. It was why she could understand why I remarried Bill— whereas you very rightly told me not to."

"How do you mean that?" Oona asked.

"Well, when Gloria falls for someone she doesn't hold even the tiniest part of herself back. She thinks and breathes and dreams that man totally. I mean, even with Bill, I know there was still some little part of myself that I kept to myself, do you know what I mean?"

"Oh, but of course—you have to."

"Well, I think then maybe you and I would always be aware of ourselves as females, you know, in relation to a man, with whatever distance that might imply. But Gloria, once she falls, just lets go of any restraint like that. I don't know whether she's right about that or not. But I know that's why she understood what I did with Bill. God, she's just been so nice to me, darling."

"Well," Oona said, "if you ask me, you're the person Gloria loves more than anyone else in the world. I mean the way she loves you makes *me* love her."

"Really?"

Oona nodded, serious and smiling.

Late into the night, Oona and Carol got around to their perennial subject, a kind of endless cornucopia of wonder and doubt, the Brown football weekend, which had taken place when they were both still in high school.

"Oona," Carol said gravely, "those boys, Jimmy and Wally, were very *bad* boys. Do you know what I mean?"

Oona couldn't help giggling.

Carol continued, with a slight smile, yet still in a grave mood, "God, that weekend was like being..."

"Orphans," Oona said.

"Oh yes," Carol said, looking directly at her friend. "Two orphans. And that was what we really were, after all, when you think about it."

The Brown Weekend
·
1938

1

THE THING ABOUT THE BROWN FOOTBALL WEEKEND WAS
that they were both going to be sensational. When they arrived
for the big gala evening after the game, even if Brown had
lost nobody would care anymore because they would never
before have seen two such beauties. It would be stunning.
The boys would never stop cutting in. And by the next morning, or almost, they would be idolized throughout the Ivy
League.

Certain boys would remember the twenty seconds or so
that they had been allowed to dance with either of them—
before the next boy cut in—for the rest of their lives. They
would be so dazzling. It wouldn't be easy to bring this off,
both of them being only fourteen. But Oona had ideas. And
Carol had ideas. Once they got to the boarding house where
Mr. Michaelson would leave them off, they'd be able to put
their heads together and check everything and make sure they
were both so beautiful that it would happen. They had to be
perfect. That was all that mattered.

Mr. Michaelson and Wally Cosgrove were talking about the
game in the front seat. Wally had a slightly puffy look but he
was terribly sweet. Since he was Jimmy Michaelson's best
friend, even though he didn't go to Brown, he was coming
up for the big weekend, his tuxedo hanging by the window.
Which one was supposed to be her date—Jimmy or Wally?
Carol had completely forgotten. It didn't matter.

"Look at the cows, darling," Oona said beside her.

They were passing some brown-and-white cows in a field. It was a beautiful day in October. Very clear and rather cold— which would be wonderful for their skin. It would bring out the roses in their cheeks. The cows looked peaceful and rather dumb. Carol wondered if these were some of the "contented," Carnation cows.

"Oona," she whispered. "Do I need pearls with my black dress—or should I wear that choker from my mother?"

"The choker."

"Right."

She patted Oona's hand absently, the question settled. There was an old farmhouse in the distance. Smoke coming out of the chimney curled into the clear blue sky, where a couple of wisps of cloud floated. Heidi could have lived there.

"Oona, I think Heidi lives there."

"Please," Oona said, starting to laugh.

"Do you think she wishes she could go to the game and be very big?"

"No, darling," Oona said. "Heidi's already internationally known. She's been immortalized."

"But I'll bet she's heard about us. Oh, Oona, I know she knows who we are."

"Of course she does, darling—through the grapevine."

They both had to exert a lot of effort not to get hysterical laughing, and cause a scene. Mr. Michaelson and Wally Cosgrove went on talking about the big football game in the front seat.

2

JIMMY MICHAELSON WAS WAITING FOR THEM IN FRONT of the old three-story boarding house on the little elm-lined street in Providence. The sidewalk was almost all covered by red and gold leaves. And Jimmy himself had red hair. He was shorter than Wally, and had a sort of quick, ferrety way about him, in contrast with his friend's more sallow, softer look.

Mr. Michaelson said goodbye to the girls in his hearty, Irish, glad-handed manner: "Well, are you two knockouts ready to be the belles of the ball?"

"Oh, I hope so, Mr. Michaelson," Carol answered with a candor so pure only Oona knew for sure that it was very funny to say so. Oona was, perhaps, the more shy. Yet their understanding of each other was so easy as to be almost telepathic.

There was another awkward moment or two, with the five of them standing beside Mr. Michaelson's navy blue Pierce Arrow in the chilly afternoon—and then the older man, having said his goodbyes, drove off. Jimmy and Wally took their bags up to a little room on the second floor. It had old-world lace and frills, doilies on the bureaus and bed rests, but outside the window was the same world of 1938, Carol mused. Daddy had talked last night at dinner about the Munich Pact, just signed by Hitler and Neville Chamberlain. Maybe there wasn't going to be another big war, after all. But he hadn't seemed very sure.

The boys told them they would pick them up at six o'clock in the waiting room downstairs for the dinner at Freed Hall. Two hours.

"It's nothing very dressy, is it?" Oona asked, as the boys were departing.

"Oh, no," said Wally.

"Oh, no," Jimmy repeated. Both of them were so serious; they must have been nervous.

"All right, we'll be ready," Carol said with a lilt of familiarity in her voice to comfort them: poor little boys who had begged Oona and her to come up for this big weekend that only *college* girls usually got to attend. And now Oona would be the talk of Brearley. And she would be the talk of Dalton. It didn't matter if the boys weren't really favorites of theirs but just two faces in the sea of boys who cut in at the tea dances and cotillions: boys they really knew only during those brief intervals before the next boy cut in. Jimmy and Wally, after all, had gone to a lot of trouble.

"See you then."

Carol closed the door as they left, and walked to the window overlooking the street, musing at the brilliant fall colors and only turning from the window as she recognized with a start that the two boys below were Jimmy and Wally leaving the boarding house.

"Darling, which one is my date?"

"I don't know," Oona answered, opening her suitcase on her bed. She lifted her evening dress out and hung it in the little pine closet.

Carol pulled her own suitcase up onto her bed.

"Have we done something terrible that we'll regret for the rest of our lives?"

Oona sat down in one of the two blue upholstered chairs, one at the foot of each bed. She crossed her legs, and then uncrossed them.

"I don't think so." She smiled. "We decided we couldn't say no even if they had two heads. Remember?"

Carol hung her own evening dress in the closet.

"A football weekend at Brown University? We couldn't, darling—could we?"

"I don't think so," Oona said, her face half in sunlight now. "Anyway, they're kind of sweet, doncha think?"

"Yes. Just shy."

In a little while, the two began to get ready for the dinner. The door of the room was opened so they could keep tabs on the use of the bathroom, which two other girls on their floor were also in and out of. As they prepared, a quickened sense of the occasion began to grow on them.

"By the way," Oona asked when they were almost ready, "who is Brown playing?"

"I think it's Harvard," Carol said, on a last trip to the bathroom.

3

WHEN THE GIRLS MADE THEIR WAY DOWNSTAIRS TO THE waiting room, they had done their very best to prepare for the evening. And having said "Good evening" to Mrs. Prescott, who owned and officiated at the boarding house—a bosomy widow in a worn muslin dress patterned with acorns, who stood at the doorway of the waiting room and said to each of the girls in turn, "Have a nice night, Miss"—neither Carol nor Oona wanted to engage in any further conversation before being picked up by Jimmy Michaelson and Wally Cosgrove.

Specifically, neither of them wanted to risk messing even an eyelash. As they entered the little waiting room, which overlooked the sidewalk, with its street lamp directly in front, there were already four other girls seated there, waiting among the lamps—two on the dark green davenport, and two on the sturdy walnut chairs, of which there were four.

As Carol took one of the remaining two chairs, she thought how sweet they all looked. Yet she and Oona—her friend sitting diagonally across the room from her—were of an entirely different order of beauty from the others, and at the same time were individual opposites.

Both wore their hair in the style Veronica Lake would later make famous—Oona brunette, Carol a blonde. In their tulle evening dresses, with shawl tops that would barely serve in the sharp night air, they were like dark and light. Oona had large eyes, almost black, that went back and back, belying her casual, almost wry manner. Looking directly into her eyes was like discovering infinity where one expected a twinkle or two. Carol's eyes, equally large, looked very brown and sat in the clear symmetry of her face like two inscrutable chocolates. Both girls had very white skin, and both wore very red lipstick.

Mrs. Prescott entered the room with a bowl of mints, which she placed on the glass-topped table in front of the davenport.

"Have a mint, girls," she said, and passed almost immediately out of the room.

One of the girls sitting directly in back of the bowl put down her copy of *Life*, with Brenda Frazier, New York's biggest debutante, on the cover, and took one of the mints in her hand, extending a pinkie as she did so. Oona and Carol locked eyes across the room, and then immediately broke the stare to avoid laughing.

It crossed Carol's mind that it might be better if Jimmy and Wally refrained from talking to them at all tonight, so that they would stay absolutely perfect. And she still wasn't sure what to do with the corsage—probably an orchid—she knew her date would bring. Corsages always seemed to ruin the dress—not to mention what was around it. They had decided that she would be Jimmy's date, Oona Wally's, unless the boys assumed it was the other way around.

Suddenly the doorbell clanged and Carol felt an electric thrill along her spine that was at least half pleasure. She had to remind herself not to get up before Jimmy and Wally entered the room. Mrs. Prescott answered the door, and two boys entered the room and this time Carol rose slightly in her chair before she realized they weren't Jimmy and Wally.

4

In another ten minutes, all of the four other girls had been picked up by their dates and the room felt like an abandoned ship. Carol and Oona stayed in their walnut chairs, though the couch would have been more comfortable, as if by some interior consent—as if their own steadfastness might impede possible disaster.

Five more minutes passed. Nothing happened at the door.

Carol looked through the window, past the white, lace-embroidered curtains, into the night. After six, it was now darker here than it was at midnight on Park Avenue. It was inky night outside—the kind of night described by Thomas Hardy, except that there were streetlights and drugstores to punctuate the darkness here. Suddenly she felt a lightness of relief, and breathed freely for perhaps the first time all day.

"Oona?"

Her friend nodded, her eyes flashing out of her own reverie.

"Oona," she said quite loudly, "it looks as if Jimmy and Wally have been killed."

"I think we should give them another five or ten minutes, darling, don't you?"

"Oh yes."

Then again, they might just be late. A flat tire maybe. Or one of them might have slipped and taken a hard fall. Or it might even be serious—a concussion perhaps. Something fell on Wally's head as he walked by—say, a large rock. It would have to be fairly heavy to begin with because the houses were all only three stories high.

They said that if you dropped a penny off the top of the

Empire State Building, by the time the penny reached the ground it had the force to kill somebody. By the time it reached the sidewalk it weighed three hundred pounds or something. It was hard to imagine. Also there was something about how, if you threw a penny off the top of the Empire State Building, and, at the same time, you threw, say, a bicycle off, they would both reach the street at exactly the same time—although you would think the bicycle, being so much heavier, would make it to the bottom faster.

"Can I get you girls anything?"

It was Mrs. Prescott, standing in the doorway.

"Oh, no thank you," Oona answered.

"Our dates are late," Carol offered.

"All right, then," said Mrs. Prescott, "I'll be in the kitchen if you need anything."

"Thank you."

If she threw Jimmy and Wally off the Empire State Building together, would they both die at exactly the same moment?

5

SUDDENLY OONA GOT UP FROM HER CHAIR AND MOVED to the davenport, where she sat down and immediately took a mint from the bowl.

"They're good," she told Carol.

Carol moved onto the couch beside her friend, and immediately tried one. It was good.

"What time is it, I wonder," Oona said.

"It's been an hour, don't you think?"

"At least."

"They could have called."

"Unless they really did get killed."

It was embarrassing. Here they were, in the middle of nowhere, both of them getting hungry now, and no one but Mrs. Prescott in sight.

"How many did you eat?" Carol asked Oona.

"Three."

"Liar."

"All right, four—maybe five."

"I get the rest then."

"What?!"

"You have two more, and I'll finish."

"I think she may have planned this bowl for the whole weekend."

"Let's eat and go back upstairs. It could be much later than we think. Somebody might even come back from their date and find us here."

The two girls sat chewing and thinking.

Having finished the bowl of mints, on their way upstairs, Carol on an impulse opened the front door, and then shut it quickly and quite hard. Then she and Oona tiptoed as quickly and quietly as possible up the stairs and into their room, and shut the door noiselessly.

"You stay on your bed," Carol whispered in the dark, "and I'll stay on mine, and maybe she won't hear us and she'll think we're having *the* most glamorous evening."

They both lay down in their evening dresses, wondering. Occasionally a car would go by outside and there would be a moment of hope—as the headlights illuminated the ceiling— but the boys would not, in the end, arrive.

It was strange, yet both girls accepted the situation with a sort of glum equanimity. It might be, after all, that this was what life was like.

Carol, having spent her earliest years in foster homes, was deeply familiar with absence as a general circumstance.

And she knew Oona, because of her father, was also no stranger to the sudden, irrational vacuum. Where were the boys? Or, in the end, *who* were the boys?

Or was there any very good reason to ask that question? They had said yes to their invitations only so that they could be beautiful and astound everybody.

Somebody, somewhere, should have phoned.

"What do you think Shane's doing?" Carol asked out of the blue.

"How should I know?" Oona answered in the dark.

"Don't you think I'd like him?"

"Oh Carol, you know he's got a girlfriend."

"Tell me about Shane, Oona."

A car went by outside: the ceiling suddenly mobile with light and shadow. Then it had passed.

The room was pleasantly warm; the radiator had been clanking when they arrived, and even now gave a sporadic hiss in the darkness.

"There's nothing to tell."

"Is he *very* handsome?"

"I guess he is. People say he is."

"But I want to know what *you* think—would I like him?"

"I think you might."

Shane lived with his girlfriend somewhere in Greenwich Village. Carol hadn't met him, but she had spoken to him on the phone. He had once phoned for Oona; and Oona, who sometimes lived with her for periods of weeks when her mother, Agnes, had a new beau and wanted the run of their apartment, had been out. So she had taken a message for her. Shane had sounded so sweet.

"I told him on the phone that I hoped to meet him sometime and he said, 'Oh, yes, I hope so too.' He did, Oona."

"I'm sure he did—and you will."

"Oona, promise me something."

"What?"

"The next time Shane phones and I pick it up—even if you're home let me say you're out, so that maybe then we'll talk some more."

141

"Okay."

"And then, see, you can call him right back and say you just got back."

"Sure."

There was quiet now in the dark room. Later in the evening, Carol heard a noise downstairs and realized she had been sleeping. She lay awake in bed for a long time, not wanting to move; then, on an impulse, she got up in the dark and undressed and put on her nightgown.

"Are you awake?"

Oona seemed to have already gotten under the covers. She got back in bed and listened again. Everything was quiet—a deeper quiet than she ever knew in New York. It must have been close to midnight. There was a clock on the dresser but it didn't glow in the dark.

6

MRS. PRESCOTT SERVED A BREAKFAST IN THE KITCHEN on the morning of the big game. The girls kept up a steady chatter about the previous evening, what they would be wearing to the game and the dance, and, in general, sustained a mood of buoyant anticipation, which Oona and Carol, though not saying very much, tried to second.

They, too, then submerged themselves in elaborate preparations for the big day, in the expectation that with the others they would be picked up for lunch. The fact that they hadn't heard from either Jimmy or Wally lay at the bottom of their thoughts like a riddle that could be solved in random ways almost at will. So they left it there and continued making themselves beautiful for the game—skirts and blouses and sweaters; scarves if they needed them.

This was the preliminary event that gave the necessary momentum to the grand finale, the big dance they would go all out for tonight. Jimmy and Wally must be somewhere because, if they weren't, if an accident had happened, Mr. Michaelson would have heard and phoned to tell them by now.

Once again, they sat in the little waiting room with the others. And again, the others were picked up within ten minutes or so, and the two found themselves alone in the room. Even Mrs. Prescott seemed to have disappeared on a midday errand somewhere. The house was suddenly so quiet that every random sound seemed to have the personal stamp of their own mood, as if they were dreaming this scene even as they sat inside it.

"Jimmy and Wally are insane."

"What are we going to do?"

"Let's kill them."

"Where *are* they?"

"I'm going to kill them when I find out. Oona, remind me to kill them."

Carol remembered long ago holding herself very still and trying to make herself as small as possible. She must have been three or four years old. She was living with a family with many children and shared a bed with two or three of them. She wanted to be taken from the bed and given her own bed and she imagined that if everything was perfect about her, this would happen. Her toes were in place; her little legs neatly plumb; her stomach, chest, shoulders, face, arms and hands and fingers all in perfectly arranged order. And no part of her was touching any part of anyone of the rest of the family. She was packed and ready to go.

It was another crisp fall day; the fall colors outside the waiting room window were ecstatic.

The way she held herself in that bed had been, maybe, her way of praying; not just with her mind, not with words which she was only beginning to understand, but with everything

143

she had—as if she had turned her whole being, from head to toe, into a message she wanted God to read.

And in the end, after all, God had answered. Her mother, who was beautiful, and sad, and loving—who loved her, she knew, from the beginning, but who didn't have any money and didn't know what to do except to be beautiful, who always smelled so good—suddenly, one day, her mother came and took her back and brought her to a home on Park Avenue, and gave her her own beautiful room, and had her sitting at the dinner table with Daddy—who really became, in his way, her father. It had happened.

Yet now she was sitting in this silent room with her friend, and it wasn't her life at all anymore. But the shadow under the door, the dust on the lamps, the little random creakings and shuttlings in and around the walls and floor—this is what she had known before her life, or what she now thought of as her life, had started.

Her mother would arrive, and hug her and kiss her and give her little toys and books. And then she would sneak away and she would be left to eat dinner with the family that had taken her in.

7

THEY SPENT THE AFTERNOON IN THEIR ROOM, NO LONGER saying very much to one another, the event of the football weekend having somehow transformed itself from a public whirlwind—the events and times listed on the itinerary they had received with their invitations, a much-handled copy of which currently lay on the glass-topped table in the waiting room—into an extended exercise in introspection: a sudden hiatus in their lives like some rainy Sunday afternoon that went on morning, noon, and night. Oona repolished her nails, fingers and toes. At one point, breaking a long silence, the two agreed that they would both have to at least *try* the new rage, black lipstick.

As the other girls began to return from the game, the excitement of Brown winning, along with the approach of the big, end-all dance, once more quickened the household. Girls made blithe, purposeful trips to the bathroom. Once more, too, Oona and Carol, on the slim chance that there was, after all, an explanation—that they hadn't, like Alice, simply dropped down a rabbit-hole that, in their case, never reached wonderland but remained only a never-ending tunnel—once again, the two got out their jars and tubes, polishes and soaps, brushes and combs, sprays and perfumes, and made themselves ready for their dates, Jimmy and Wally. Tonight, in fact, as planned long in advance, the two had decided to carry out an unprecedented experiment. They would both wear a perfume they had been saving for just the right moment, the perfume by Schiaparelli called "Shocking."

The waiting room this time was like some extraordinary aviary: everyone dressed and coiffed and made up and perfumed to the extreme of their individual limits. Even now, Carol found herself touched by so bright and hopeful a display of plumage. These were, after all, eternal mating rites being enacted in their own contemporary setting, and these girls all caught something of the ancient flame. Just the sideways glance of the girl who had held the mint with her pinky out, a not un-nice girl, after all, but one who definitely let the mascara run away with her—somehow, the very exaggeration now around her eyes was like a flash of the goddess.

Oona, of course, sat in their midst like Athena herself. Her beauty, with its sudden, galvanizing intensity, appeared to operate like a primal law to which Oona herself seemed innocently oblivious—a law like gravity, or magnetism. What would happen to her quiet, almost scholarly nature amidst such a force?

The same four boys came to pick up the same four girls, and left the same two girls alone in the room. This was it, the big night of the big weekend—and Jimmy and Wally were not going to come, and were not going to phone, and they were going to be left to go crazy, two doomed hostages of a lunatic Ivy League.

"I'm starving, Carol."

"So am I."

"We can go eat. I'm completely out of candy bars. Let's. Let's get out of here, darling."

"If we wear our raincoats," Carol said, "nobody'll notice we're wearing evening dresses. And if we happen to run into those two, they can take us to the dance—after we kill them."

8

So it happened that on the gala evening Oona and Carol had so long plotted, planned, and looked forward to—imagining the dancing, the boys, the whirlwind of romance and glory—the two girls ended up sneaking out of the boarding house in their raincoats (over their embroidered and encrusted silk off-the-shoulder evening dresses) and out into the chill, starry night to see what was going on.

They walked down several residential blocks together in near silence—a sliver of moon was hanging at one far end of the sky—and then spotted a neighborhood corner drugstore. Entering this brightly lit, festive haven, they immediately felt relief bordering on joy. They bought movie magazines (Frances Farmer, Errol Flynn) and candy bars (Powerhouse, Jujubes) and various makeup accoutrements, making both of their pocketbooks swell. Before leaving, Carol caught sight of the headline on the Saturday *Providence Journal*: "BRITISH LORD OF ADMIRALTY RESIGNS OVER MUNICH PACT." Was there going to be a war, or what?

Outside again, standing beneath the corner street lamp, they looked as far as possible in one direction, and then in another, and then began to walk in the direction they thought might lead into the campus. In five minutes they were walking through the Brown quadrangle; the building where the dance was being held was unmistakably lit up and the obvious source of the muted dance music on the surrounding air.

Carol stopped for a moment, touching Oona's hand to let her know. She was suddenly furious.

"I don't believe this is happening!"

"What if they're inside? We can't go in."

"I know . . . But we've got to look. Don't you want to?"

"Oh yes. I just hope nobody sees us or recognizes us or anything."

"Oh no. They won't, Oona. Don't worry."

The two walked purposefully across the quadrangle, and then more stealthily beside the large red brick building itself. The band was playing "It Was Just One of Those Things." The windows were set a bit higher than either of them could see through. Near the corner of the building, Carol left the paved walkway and went behind a large holly bush—so that she was now directly under a window—and put her pocketbook down on the ground. Oona came in beside her. They stood together in the darkness for a moment, both slightly breathless. Carol put her hand on the window ledge just above her head.

"I can give you a lift," Oona said, putting her pocketbook down too.

Oona laced her fingers together. Carol hesitantly put her foot into the stirrup Oona made with her hands.

"Really, darling, it's all right."

"Okay, I just want to make sure no one's coming."

There didn't seem to be any passersby on the horizon. Carol

put both hands on the window ledge and lifted herself, as Oona supported her.

"Are you okay?" she whispered. She could see her own breath fogging the window pane. She felt the light on her face.

"Fine, fine," her friend whispered below.

9

THE ROOM WAS HUGE—A GYMNASIUM DECORATED WITH colored paper streamers and balloons—and there were lots of couples dancing in their tuxedos and evening gowns. The band looked larger than any she'd seen at cotillions.

Carol made a quick, almost involuntary scan of the faces of the hundred or so boys, half hoping and half dreading that she would spot Wally or Jimmy. But neither one of them turned up. However, in the midst of this survey, she stalled momentarily on a face she recognized. He was standing with his date by a table soliciting donations for the "Musicians Emergency Fund."

"Oh, Oona!" she whispered, excited and hunching down toward her. "Guess who's here? Billy Harbach, remember Billy?"

"Of course."

"Oh, he looks so handsome."

After another look, Carol got down and the two exchanged positions so that Oona could have a turn at the window, her features suddenly illuminated by the window's light.

"Sort of over by the right, near the donation table," Carol whispered, holding her firmly aloft by her stockinged foot.

As her friend scanned the festivities, the band struck up "Umbrella Man."

"Oh, I see him!"

"Isn't he handsome?"

"Yes!"

"He's with kind of a dog, though, doncha think? Oh, Oona, I think someone's coming!" Carol whispered urgently.

Oona let herself down quickly, and the two stood side by side, each in their stockinged feet only a little over five feet tall, and both breathing heavily, as a couple from the dance strolled by, making a lot of clicking noises with their heels. After they had passed, and the two put their pumps back on, Carol moved out from behind the holly bush, looked around, and then moved onto the pavement and Oona quickly followed.

They began to walk swiftly and they kept a quickened pace until they were all the way across the quadrangle. Carol stopped now beside a street lamp, watching the little gilt specks that flashed in the sidewalk.

"Let's catch our breath. If we'd gone just a little faster we'd have been flying."

Oona laughed, breathless too.

When the two arrived back at the boarding house later that night, they looked in the waiting room window from the sidewalk to make sure none of the other girls were saying goodnight to their beaus. Then they opened and closed the front door as quietly as possible and snuck upstairs to their room. Before either of them had time to hang up her evening gown, another girl arrived back and made a lot of noise saying goodnight and climbing the stairs.

10

A SUNDAY GOODBYE BRUNCH ON THE CAMPUS HAD BEEN planned, and Carol and Oona, with orphans' pride, dutifully appeared in the waiting room with the others at eleven o'clock the next morning. When the four other girls had been picked up, they waited another five minutes and then, with Mrs. Prescott out of view, went quickly back upstairs (Oona had counted exactly eighteen steps) and into their room. Each settled on her bed with one of the movie magazines they had picked up the night before at the drugstore. Eventually they both fell asleep and neither of them woke up again until the girls began to return from the brunch.

After getting up, Carol and Oona, both a bit groggy with the midday nap, got out their suitcases and packed. Mr. Michaelson would be picking them up at three o'clock to drive them back to New York, and he had asked them to wait outside for him unless they had their first snow. As the hour drew near, the two girls made their way downstairs, each in her raincoat and gripping her suitcase. After saying their goodbyes to Mrs. Prescott—"Goodbye. Come again, Miss," the old woman said to each of them, shaking their hands—they waited beside their suitcases outside on the sidewalk in front of the house. It was overcast and cold. Neither knew quite what to expect now but, in fact, Mr. Michaelson's Pierce Arrow appeared in front of the house almost exactly at three. The robust Irishman with his permanently ruddy cheeks waved to them jovially from the car and got out.

Then, suddenly, everything went crazy. As Mr. Michaelson was unlocking the trunk where he would put the suitcases,

Jimmy and Wally both appeared around the corner, and ran over. Their arrival coincided almost exactly with Mr. Michaelson's stepping up to the sidewalk to take Oona's and Carol's suitcases. Jimmy immediately took Oona's suitcase himself, heading with it toward the back trunk as Mr. Michaelson headed over with Carol's, and Wally carried his tuxedo on its hanger and hung it up—as on the ride up—by the back window.

After Mr. Michaelson had arranged the two bags in the back trunk, he turned a knowing smile on all of them, and then focused on Oona and Carol, who stood with helpless half-smiles before the older man's glorious assumptions, much like their own of two days before.

"Well," he said, "did you two belles have the time of your life? Now tell me."

"Oh, it was great!" Wally suddenly piped up, his hair somewhat askew in back, but apparently in full possession of his faculties.

"Oh, yes—wonderful!" Jimmy chimed in now; Jimmy with red hair, and little eyes smiling warmly at both of them.

"All right, boys—but let's hear it from the gals, shall we? How was it, then, you dazzlers?"

It was absolutely absurd. Here they were with these two lying, thieving, crummy, two-faced little horrors who had, indeed, given them the time of their life, and this big, happy, innocent father of one of the boys and, somehow, they just ... *couldn't*.

"Oh, yes, it was wonderful," Carol said in a softer than normal voice.

"Oh, yes," Oona seconded, with a slight hesitation. "Marvelous."

"Didn't I tell you?" Mr. Michaelson went on, aglow with the triumph. "Dazzlers. The two of them. Two dazzlers."

151

11

On the ride home, Wally again sat in the front with Mr. Michaelson and the two discussed the game. Carol and Oona were quieter than they had been on the ride up— scarcely exchanging a word during the whole two-hour drive. Near the end of it, just before he dropped both girls off, Mr. Michaelson turned around in his seat at a red light at Fiftieth Street and Park Avenue. It was just dark in the city. As the lights of traffic played across his face, making his large features almost indiscernible, he addressed Carol and Oona: "Well, you two have been awfully quiet for having enchanted an entire university."

"We're just tired," Carol answered, aware that at least she wasn't telling another *total* lie. She was exhausted.

Then, at 420 Park Avenue, Mr. Michaelson got out of the car to open the back trunk. Wally stayed in the front seat, saying a muted "Goodbye" and barely turning around as Carol and Oona got out of the back. The two answered him with the same word, but they both gave it an unmistakable undercurrent of deeper, more final meaning.

"Well, girls," Mr. Michaelson said enthusiastically as the three stood on the lit-up sidewalk under the building's awning and John, the doorman, moved past them, taking their suitcases to the elevator, "let's do this again real soon, shall we?"

"Wonderful," Carol answered, unable to help liking this old fool.

"Yes," said Oona, looking very intently at a fire hydrant, "let's."

Fat chance.

12

THAT NIGHT, IN CAROL'S BEDROOM, OONA SITTING ON the twin bed she used while Carol sat Indian-style on her own, the two made a solemn pact that no one would know the truth—ever. They would go back to school the next morning with stories of the greatest football weekend in history—of triumph, glory, and shimmering romance—and make themselves the envy of everyone they knew. And, with their individual stories carefully cross-checked, that is what they did.

Having come through this trial by fire together with a secret only the two of them could share, Carol and Oona would be friends for life. In the years to come, after marriages and children, in their various houses, late at night after everyone else had gone to sleep, the two would sit up together and sooner or later, as on this night in Nice, the conversation would always come around to the Brown weekend, and they would end up discussing what might have happened that would explain it. One year they decided that Jimmy and Wally must have been having a passionate affair with each other, a supposition with the incidental interest that it would have been completely inconceivable to either of them at the time. Later on, it occurred to them that maybe the two had ended up, as boys were sometimes known to do, getting drunk and then— one or the other, or both of them—getting sick from it. And so they would miss one, or perhaps even two of the events. And then maybe they hadn't had the nerve to show up again until the end. This was the story that finally, over the years, came to seem the most plausible.

Neither Carol nor Oona ever saw or heard a word about

either Jimmy Michaelson or Wally Cosgrove ever again, a circumstance that proved to be fairly unique. Years later, Carol occasionally would see Billy Harbach, whom they had glimpsed through the gymnasium window, at a Hollywood party. He had become a television producer.

The Sound of Love
·
1957

1

Carol woke up the next morning in Nice to the sound of the Chaplin children departing for the beach. There was a motor idling, various voices in last-minute urgencies— she recognized thirteen-year-old Geraldine's: "I forgot my book!"—a car door slamming, two more slams, and then the creep of tires over gravel. That wonderful noise, so cozy somehow. She turned on her side, gathering the covers up tighter around her. The sun was already high—a luminous orange fringe of climbing nasturtiums edged the French doors leading to her terrace—but there was still a little morning breeze, carrying on it some indefinable, slightly rank extra—an essence of the beach.

Carol closed her eyes and saw the colors darken a few degrees. Now they were inside her, as though she'd swallowed them. Like vitamins. How did you explain the fact that some people—Oona and Charlie, for instance—seemed to understand everything and always do everything right, and the weather is perfect, and the food is marvelous, and their love is in bloom, and the birds are expressing themselves outside the windows right now?

It wasn't just the fact that Charlie was a genius. No, because so was O'Neill, wasn't he? And so, supposedly, was Bill. At least when she married him he was supposed to be. Grounds for divorce? His genius is gone, your honor. And he's lost his *joie de vivre*. His *esprit de corps*, I can testify, was all a big act.

"Non!" Somehow the judge was a Frenchman, young, thin-featured—it was Elinor's ex-husband, Henri—and he was looking down at her with obvious shock. He reached into his robes and brought out a package of Gauloises, shook some cigarettes up from the package and offered her one, leaning down from the podium.

She opened her eyes again. Poor Henri and Elinor. More out of her own mold. She sat up in bed now and looked out at the room, with its white walls and dark wood trim, and those perfect blue French Provincial fabrics. Elinor said she had fallen in love with him on the dance floor. She lost her mind to the music in his arms. These things happened all the time. Now she was on Fire Island with Hubert and Annie, and Henri was back in Paris. Maybe he'd run into Aram and Lucy and Bill, who were in Europe for the summer.

There was a light knock on her door, and she pulled the covers up around her.

"Yes?"

"Breakfast, madame?" It was a young woman's voice; the door remained unopened.

"Oh, yes," she said.

Now the door opened and a pretty young girl with long black hair and dark eyebrows carried a tray across the room and through the French doors out onto the terrace. She arranged a coffee pot and a plate and some smaller items, and then set the doors ajar.

"Thank you," Carol said.

"Oui, madame," she answered with a quick smile and nod as she walked back through the room carrying the white tray painted with flowers. She shut the door.

Carol retrieved her nightgown from the foot of the bed and slipped it on, and then got up from the bed and put on the blue Porthault robe Oona had left for her last night. She walked out onto the terrace in her bare feet.

Below and beyond a number of other villas, each with its terraced garden, you could see the beach, and sailboats here and there on the blue, blue water.

She sat down at the little white cast-iron table. There were warm croissants and cups of butter and jelly, a sugar bowl, and a pot of coffee and a pitcher of cream. As she ate her breakfast, she breathed deeply, taking in all the little flutterings of noise and light and shade. She'd read somewhere of birdsong that it was the way each bird declared a certain territory to be its own. Little environments of noise supposed to protect their places, their perches. Their voices, little homes.

She buttered a croissant and added strawberry preserves from the little cup, sipped her coffee with cream and sugar. A cardinal swooped low through the garden—like a sudden, moving piece of air—and lighted on a branch of a lemon tree in the corner of the garden. Then, for the first time, she heard *consciously* a sound she had been hearing off and on amongst the birds and the flutterings of the leaves. It was Charlie, laughing.

She listened intently now and distinguished Oona's voice—the rhythm of it, rather, since she couldn't quite make out the words: that slightly clipped intonation, a little edge in the way she spoke, her slightly sidewise manner. She remembered the way Oona, in contrast to Gloria, had advised her against a second marriage to Bill: simply, "He's impossible." Period.

And there was Charlie's laughter again.

She realized they were having their breakfast where they had all had dinner last night: the terrace that, in fact, was right below *her* terrace. Here she was, then, unwittingly become an eavesdropper on a marriage that had assumed, over the years, the status of legend.

It was strange, so full of extraordinary coincidences, the way things had worked out for her and Gloria and Oona. She met Bill when she went to California to be bridesmaid at Gloria's wedding to Pat di Cicco. And Oona, in turn, met Charlie after she accompanied Carol to Sacramento so she could see Bill during his basic training. It had been the occasion of Bill's and her first big disaster, which had triggered

Oona's and her unanticipated departure for Los Angeles, where Oona met Charlie.

Bill had booked Oona and her into a small suite at the Senator Hotel in Sacramento while she waited for the first day he would be allowed to have a visit. Carol and Oona were both eighteen and spent the interim days at the hotel reading movie magazines, taking bubble baths, gossiping, and going out to the White Tower for hamburgers and french fries and Cokes. Oona had written to her father, hoping she could visit him while she was on the West Coast with Carol, but he had sent her a horrible letter from Tao House in Contra Costa County. O'Neill was apparently furious at Oona for being chosen Debutante of the Year by the Stork Club in New York. He had some kind of phobia about anything that hinted of show business, and apparently immediately assumed some terrible compromise of his name by Oona, which was ridiculous. And so, for really the first time in either of their lives, they were absolutely on their own. And loving it.

They had gotten to Sacramento together, oddly enough, by way of Carol's mother. When Bill called long-distance from the West Coast and spoke to Rosheen to say he wanted Carol to come out to California to meet his family, and all but asked for Carol's hand in marriage, Rosheen, immediately assuming her portable English accent, insisted that of course her eighteen-year-old daughter would have to have a chaperone.

Bill, who appeared to be one hundred percent serious, immediately consented. But when her mother hung up and had a chance to review the situation, she realized there was no one to send with Carol except the housekeeper, and she couldn't spare her. For one thing, Daddy would be annoyed. So Carol convinced her that *Oona* could be chaperone—which was a bit like sending the Katzenjammer Kids on a mission of high propriety. The two of them together somehow failed to enforce the starched aura she knew Rosheen had in mind.

The one problem she and Oona had to deal with at the Senator Hotel was Bill's request that, until he could see her at the army base, Carol write him a letter each day. Maybe because it was *all* she had to think about, she let it balloon into an obsession—what should she write him? After all, he was a famous American writer, and what if she wrote him something that wasn't very intelligent? Would he decide he didn't want to marry her?

The two girls discussed the situation one afternoon as they left their room and then waited for the elevator down to the lobby. They were going to the White Tower a few blocks away. They stood beside the marble spittoon by the elevator doors.

"Oona, you're the intelligent one—tell me what to write."

"Darling, I'm not. No more than you. Really."

The elevator doors opened and they got on with a middle-aged couple and a young man in uniform with so close a crew cut that you could see several moles on his scalp. They both remained silent until they got to the lobby. Loud music greeted them as the elevator doors opened. There was a military band in the middle of the lobby and everyone had stood up and was singing to the music:

> Praise the lord and pass the ammunition
> Praise the lord and swing into position

Frank Loesser. My God, it had really been another world, suddenly, that fall of 1942. America finally getting all the way into the war, another *mood*, suddenly, and one Bill would never quite comprehend or accept as valid. And, in a certain sense, this was really the beginning of the end of his career as a literary high-roller because he refused whatever the personal stretch involved might have been.

Over hamburgers at the White Tower, Oona had an idea. She had just gotten a long and witty letter from Jerry Salinger, the young writer she knew in New York—she'd told Carol

159

she summarily socked him in the jaw one night when he got too romantic—and they could use some of the witty lines from his letter in Carol's letters to Bill.

"What kind of lines?" Carol asked her, looking out the picture window at the Main Street traffic. It was overcast.

"Oh, I don't know. Things like 'I've just sent my typewriter to the laundry.'"

"Oo," Carol said with a surge of excitement, "that's *very* witty. Oh, Oona, Bill's going to think I'm a genius."

So they rushed back to the hotel room. And Carol got out hotel stationery and sat down at the little desk in their room and Oona sat down Indian-style on her bed with the letter, marking and calling out all the witty lines to Carol. She wrote a page for each day during the next hour and peppered them all with the Salinger witticisms. She was delighted with herself. Now Bill would realize just how extraordinary a girl he was going to marry.

It was at the army base that it all went haywire with Bill— that first afternoon he was allowed to have visitors. She, along with a crowd of other girlfriends, wives, family, and friends, was there at the big Rec Room on the base. Bill's first look at her was the giveaway. He looked ... preoccupied. As though, although this meeting was the culmination of a week-long wait for the two of them, there was something else on his mind. He greeted her without so much as a kiss.

"Hello, kid."

"Hello."

They stood amidst the crowd of other pairs and groups throughout the room.

"Muggy, isn't it?" Bill *never* commented on the weather.

"Bill, has something happened? Did I—did I do something wrong?"

"Let's go across the street, kid—at least we'll have a little privacy over there."

He took her across the street into some kind of office. They chatted in a stilted way a moment longer among the desks and typewriters.

Finally, he told her.

"It was those fucking letters. Christ, I thought you were just a sweet, innocent young kid, and now I find out you're another one of these clever, literary women. Jesus, I hate all that crap."

"Oh, but Bill..." Her heart was racing; she had to break through her own deception. "...I didn't write those..."

"Look, kid, don't lie about it. Because if there's anything in the world that I hate more than a clever, literary woman, it's a goddamn liar."

So she and Oona boarded a train from Sacramento to Los Angeles that evening, figuring they might as well visit a girl-friend there while they were on the West Coast. Everything was over. Carol was numb. But Oona ended up meeting Char-lie a few weeks later in Los Angeles because of the way things had gone. It was like magic; like all the things they had talked about for years sitting on the twin beds on Park Avenue—a screen test, and some kind of instant chemistry between them: Oona had told her later that it was like meeting the hand-somest, sexiest man in the world. Of course, they'd *all* gotten what they dreamed of as girls—only in Oona's case it was real.

The postscript was that after Carol's *second* marriage to Bill in 1951 in Beverly Hills, she and Bill took a honeymoon cruise to Catalina with Charlie and Oona on their yacht. It was spring and Bill kept reading a new novel they had on board, and every so often he'd look up and say things like "This kid's really got it," and "Now here's a real writer, for God's sake."

"You didn't think so in Sacramento," Oona said to him with a smile at one point. But that was the sort of comment Bill barely heard. He was too caught up enjoying *The Catcher in the Rye*.

There it was again—Charlie's laughter. Then, silence for a moment—or rather the variety of garden noises... and now that intonation she recognized as Oona's again.

A little blue mail truck appeared down the Chaplins' drive-way and puttered up to the entrance. The jaunty young mail-man, wearing his postal uniform with navy blue short pants, got out and sprinted to the door with a stack of mail for the Chaplins. Oona and Charlie would be getting it all at their breakfast, she supposed.

Everything in its proper place—God, the sheer force of mind or energy or whatever it was that could put a life together like Charlie and Oona had, full of the real pleasures of life. That was what Daddy had done, too—at least for a few years of her own life, even if it seemed he was never quite fulfilled in his marriage.

And again then: Charlie's laughter. It occurred to Carol it was the sound of love—of a man's wholehearted appreciation of his wife. Oona had found the life all of them sought.

Carol had six full days of rest and enjoyment with the Chaplins before going on to Paris, where she stayed at the St. Regis and spent two days walking through the city by herself. Then she got a call from Elinor in New York. She had to come home because Bill had delivered Aram and Lucy back to New York earlier than the date agreed on for their summer vaca-tions. There was no argument possible. The children were at Ninety-third Street. Elinor was taking care of them until Carol got home. She got the first plane back to New York.

2

Walking out of the passenger tunnel from the plane into the La Guardia terminal, she saw Walter smiling at her from one side of the little group waiting for passengers on her flight. It was the one face, she knew with a sort of instantaneous, half-articulated joy, that brought some kind of peace to her own heart. You couldn't explain that one, probably. But you could feel it.

"Darling, it's so good to see you."

She kissed him with a sudden surge of feeling, which he returned in kind.

"Hiya, pussycat. How was the continent?" he asked her, letting his voice go very English on the last two words. He hugged her tightly for a moment.

"It was just ... oh, darling, what are you doing here? How did you know when I was coming?"

"I'll tell ya about it, sweetheart. Elinor told me. I'm out on Fire Island with my kids and Gerry. I've gotta catch a plane in about twenty minutes. I'm going out to the coast to do an 'Alfred Hitchcock Presents.' Let's sit down and have a drink or a sandwich or something."

"Umm." In that first rush of seeing him again, she'd almost forgotten he was a married man, the father of a boy and a girl, David and Jenny.

So it was the old mess of her life again. By the time she got into New York in a taxi, it was a rusty, dank summer twilight, but—oh boy—it was still New York. And that meant that even if you were nuts, which she surely was, there were plenty of others who were also nuts and the trick of it all was to keep going, notice Madison Avenue, so quiet on a summer evening. Get out, pay the driver, and into the front door of the building. Get up the elevator. Into the apartment. Aram, who looked a little different, she couldn't quite say how, could go downstairs for her other two bags.

By midnight, when the children were finally down in their beds, she was finding her way back into the little corners and comforts of her own room—the living room by day; *her* room by this time each night. So, the kids had had their summer with their father. Lucy seemed fine; Aram, she suspected, had been hearing horror stories about her from Bill. That was, of course, a game that two could play—but she knew she wouldn't be playing it. Or she hoped she wouldn't be. The kids had been uprooted and displaced enough as it was without having to contend with their parents' need to continue their old arguments in their children's minds and hearts. She would have to see.

3

KEN TYNAN, WHOM SHE SOMEHOW ASSUMED SHE WOULD never see again, called the first week she was back to tell her he'd come to New York to live—he was going to be the theater critic for *The New Yorker*. And he had plans for her.

"I'm going to give you something vital," he said on the phone that first evening, "—a political conscience."

"Oh, I thought it was going to be something more interesting."

"Like what, my darling?"

"Oh, just something silly. With diamonds."

"You astonish me. You and Bertolt Brecht. I saw *Mother*

Courage in Berlin. My God, that's genius. That, and you."

"Whatever you say—but I can't marry you."

"Why?"

"Because you're a theater critic."

"There's a logic there. I'm certain of it. But it's one that speeds ahead of my dying brain."

"Do you want a Dexamyl?"

"Divine. A blond American divinity. Like Marilyn."

He took her to a Greek restaurant on Lexington Avenue one night and told her all about *Mother Courage*. The soldiers come to take her children away and she gives them such a smile. He said it was one of the most thrilling moments he had ever known in the theater.

It made her remember a scene in *The Iceman Cometh*, which she had seen years ago, around the time she met Bill. It was the scene where the character named Hickey takes away all the drinkers' pipe dreams. One of the men he tears down— it was the part played by an actor named Dudley Digges, whom Ken said he knew of—walks off the stage then as if he were naked, as if his heart had been broken.

She remembered that at the time she thought it must have been a mistake, what he did. Oh, there was a moment or two in a whole lifetime, maybe, when you actually saw something like that. It was like glancing into someone's soul instead of a face, and she herself had seen it once or twice—in the face of a girl who worked in a flower shop near the Plaza Hotel one summer during the war—but even then it seemed like an accident. Or perhaps, as she had suspected with Dudley Digges, something she only *thought* she saw. Except that she went back to the play a week later and saw it again. She had to find out and she was still at home with Daddy and her mother, and it was a play by Eugene O'Neill, after all. So they let her go again. And Dudley Digges did it again. He had done it on purpose.

165

Well, after all, maybe the theater was there, maybe all art was there, to show you the secrets of people you couldn't grasp in the usual crush of the daily round: everything went by too fast. And so you came to sit in an audience one night and watch an actor or actress turn themselves inside out, and you went away with your heart younger than it had been when you came to the theater. Love, of course, was the other thing that could do that to you.

4

WALTER CAME BACK FROM THE WEST COAST AND THEY started seeing one another again. And then she got a job as Anne Baxter's understudy in *The Square Root of Wonderful* by Carson McCullers. She wasn't sure Anne didn't think it was supposed to be some kind of reprise of *All About Eve* with the desperate young ingenue waiting in the wings for her chance to upstage the movie star, but she was really just making a living. Aram was going to Trinity now, and doing poorly because he loved photography more than school work and Dick Avedon had given him an after-school job in his studio. Lucy was at Dalton and doing quite well. Bill sent money for their schools, but no child support. Thank God for Mr. Novick, the sweet man who was the manager of her local Gristede's market. He had known her since she was a girl—he had been her mother's grocer—and he went on extending her credit, even though she owed him over a thousand dollars now.

Every night she went to her job, and afterwards she would meet Walter for coffee and they'd walk to his little apartment on Central Park West or back to Ninety-third Street.

"How are you, darling?" she asked him one evening over

coffee at the Calico Kitchen when he seemed a little down.

"I'm fine, sweetheart," he said, looking up with a sort of open-eyed, boyish curiosity at the question itself. *"Very* good," he went on, as if amused at his own circumstances, "for a man who owes his bookie three thousand dollars and wants to be married to a different woman than the one he's married to..."

"Oh, darling," Carol answered, "I hope you're not just saying that to make me feel good."

Walter's smile moved into his eyes.

Soon after *The Square Root of Wonderful* closed, she started a long series of auditions for a part she really wanted: Myra in S. N. Behrman's *The Cold Wind and the Warm,* based on his own book *The Worcester Account,* which she'd read in installments in *The New Yorker.* It seemed to be snowing, or to have just snowed, most of the time now. The city looked so lovely in the snow, each thing—the stoplight, the fire hydrant—with its unifying stripe of white.

The problem was that the director, Harold Clurman, wanted his girlfriend to have the part. But Mr. Behrman apparently liked *her* and so they kept calling her back. Harold, of course, was hoping Mr. Behrman would get tired of her. He was trying to "read her out," but it seemed to work the other way.

One afternoon after she'd read again, the playwright very warmly said hello to her.

"I understand you have two children," he said.

"Oh, yes," she answered, startled at the question, "I do." It wasn't the sort of thing you advertised in the theater, especially when you were reading for the part of an ingenue barely out of her teens—really Behrman's dream-memory of his first love.

"How old are they?" asked the venerable old man with no thought in the world, she knew, except polite conversation.

"Oh, two and three," she said quickly. Aram was fourteen and Lucy twelve.

She got the part. And Ken Tynan reviewed her in *The New Yorker*, saying she "pitched Myra somewhere between a pallid fawn and a Southern belle." She didn't know whether that was a compliment or not.

5

THAT WINTER WALTER WENT TO TIJUANA TO GET A DI-vorce. As it happened, Bill came to town the day Walter got back. Walter had a long-standing date to take Aram, who was only barely coming out of the emotional fog about her that Bill seemed to have cast him into during the summer in Europe, to a Knicks game. That evening—it was late February now, still gray and cold—the buzzer rang at the Ninety-third Street apartment and it was Aram, asking if he could bring Pop up for a minute. She really couldn't refuse him that. But then, only a moment later, the buzzer rang again and it was Walter. So, now Bill and Walter were going to meet. Possibly in the elevator.

She opened the front door of the apartment and stood waiting for the arrivals. The elevator stopped on their floor and she heard Walter inside the elevator speaking to Bill.

"Yeah, Bill, I always thought you were a taller feller."

Her heart sank. She knew Walter hadn't meant anything by it, but it was the sort of comment that would enshrine him on Bill's personal dart board for all time. They all arrived together, the three of them, Bill and Walter and Aram, all of them smiling, all a little awkward at their impromptu conjunction.

Inside, in the living room, she gave Bill a cup of coffee while Walter had a beer. He reminded Aram of the game they were going to, and then left the room for a moment to make a call on the phone in the hall in front of the back bedrooms.

After Walter had left the room, Bill actually said to Aram, "Now, don't feel that you have to go, son," referring to the basketball game Walter was taking him to.

"Oh, no, Pop," Aram answered, eating a hamburger Carol had brought him at the round gray marble table in the corner of the room, "I *want* to go."

"All right, my boy."

Then Walter returned to the living room, and he and Aram got on their coats to go.

"Nice to meet you, Bill," Walter said, smiling and shaking his hand.

"Nice to meet *you*, Walter," Bill said. And then, looking at Aram, "Goodbye, my boy."

"Goodbye, Pop."

She got ready for the theater while Bill spent a little time with Lucy as she ate her dinner in the living room. Lucy loved Bill so much it frightened Carol. "My tumbling tumbleweed!" he'd call her, and laugh and hug her tightly. And then he'd be gone from her life after a day or two.

That night, inside the taxi Carol and Bill shared downtown—she would be dropping him off at the Great Northern on West Fifty-seventh Street on her way to her theater, the Belasco—he turned to her. She had known he would, of course.

"So, it's Matthau, hunh, kid?" he said.

"Yes, Bill, it is."

"A married man."

"He's not married, Bill."

"You're still a liar, hunh?"

"He's not married, Bill."

She insisted and he insisted most of the ride downtown through the nighttime, still slush-edged streets. She certainly didn't owe him the revelation that Walter had gotten his divorce within the last twenty-four hours. What for? She told him the truth, and that was *all* she owed him. If, in fact, she even owed him that.

The week after *The Cold Wind and the Warm* closed, she and Maureen Stapleton, who played the lead, were invited by Bob Whitehead, the producer, to a dinner for Mr. Behrman at "21."

"And how are your children?" Mr. Behrman asked her solicitously at one point.

"Oh, they're fine," Carol replied, her heart immediately jumping into her throat. "Fine," she added again, her voice almost clotted in an attempt to be casual.

"Yes," Mr. Behrman went on, "I understand your son is remarkable. He's the only three-year-old who edits his high school literary magazine."

They all laughed, as she herself finally did, too. Some dirty rat had told him.

———————————————

6

———————————————

ONE EVENING IN LATE SPRING—RIGHT AFTER DAYLIGHT savings time, so it was light again till almost eight at night—Carol and Walter, neither of whom had a job at the moment, were walking down Fifty-seventh Street and passed the Great Northern Hotel, where Carol knew Bill liked to stay. (He had written *The Time of Your Life* there in six days and kept his warm associations with the place even as it declined.) As they headed east toward the corner of Sixth Avenue, approaching the Automat in the middle of the block, she was about to remark to Walter that Bill always liked to eat at the Automat, when suddenly she saw her ex-husband sitting with another man at one of the tables in the picture window at the front of the cafeteria.

"Oh my God, I think that's Bill."

"In the Automat?"

"Yes—oh, don't look! He'll see us."

"Sweetheart, he's your ex-husband. Not an SS officer."

"Oh, you're right, darling," she said, holding Walter's arm tighter and picking up her pace. "But do me a favor and don't look."

"Whatever you say, pussycat."

They continued toward the corner of Sixth Avenue, the evening sky still blue through the wide corridor of Fifty-seventh Street. They passed a construction site, closed up for the day.

"When I was young," Walter told her, "I used to like to watch the fellas working—whatta they call em? People who watch the men working?"

"Transients?"

Walter laughed his silent, appreciative laugh.

As they approached the corner, Carol began to unclench from the near encounter with Bill. Then, just as she was feeling safely beyond his orbit, suddenly, there he was, along with another man, perhaps the one he'd been sitting with at the Automat, walking briskly up Sixth Avenue, from the direction of Fifty-sixth Street, toward them.

"Well," Bill said in his booming voice as their paths were about to cross, and with a jovial look at the two of them, "if you walk around in New York long enough, sooner or later you meet your family."

"Hiya, Bill," Walter said to him, smiling.

"Hello, Walter, old buddy."

"Hello, Bill." She made herself smile. It was absurd, but she suddenly felt rather calm.

"Well, it's a beautiful evening for a walk."

"Yes, it is," she answered.

171

Let him work this one out.

"I'm going to call the kids. I just got into town."

"Wonderful."

"All right, now, you two have a good walk. Dickran and I have some very important business to attend to right down the street here at the Automat. Right, Dickran?"

The man, a small, compact Armenian with a dour look, brightened slightly and replied, "Right, Bill."

They continued on their way.

"Don't tell me you think I'm crazy," Carol said to Walter on the other side of Sixth Avenue, "I swear to you it was him in the window of the Automat."

"Oh, no," Walter told her as Carol slowed down to look at pocketbooks in Bendel's windows, "I believe you. I think maybe Bill still cares about you. Jesus, he must have made that guy hustle to get all the way around the block like that."

Carol giggled. "Oh, I can just see him making that poor man run."

"But what I want to know," Walter went on, as they picked up the pace again, "—what I want to know is what do they call those people who watch them work at construction sites?"

"Bums?"

Walter laughed again without laughing out loud. They continued then, arm in arm, to the corner of Fifth Avenue.

"Loiterers," he said suddenly, breaking a silence neither had noticed. "They call them loiterers. Remember that one for your writing. It's a good one for your vocabulary."

"Oh, I will, darling. Don't worry. I will."

7

Apparently Ken Tynan called one afternoon and left a message for her with Aram. But she never got it (she found the folded piece of paper with his scrawled message in the pocket of one of his pairs of jeans as she was getting the laundry together a week or so later). Then Ken called her again.

"I must see you."

"Ken, please. You know I'm involved with someone else."

"That has nothing to do with it and it doesn't matter in the slightest. Give Walter my regards. I think he may be the best character actor in America."

"How 'bout just plain best actor?"

"Fine, fine, but I must see you. One hour."

"One hour?"

"That's right. Just an hour."

"One hour . . . would be okay."

What was it all about? They would get together so he could recharge his battery for romantic fantasy? Yes, he was fun to be with, and it was terribly flattering, of course. And deep in her bones, she knew he was really only involved with her in the most peripheral sort of way, whatever his protestations.

"All right," she said in the end, "I'll see you. But I'm going to bring my alarm clock and in *exactly* one hour I'm leaving."

Why not take him at his word and focus the relationship to its highest concentration, in the shortest possible time frame? If it was a time-bomb, it would go off; but she knew it was only a peanut. And she didn't want to spend a lot of time hovering over it. What was this supposed to be, anyway? Existentialism?

She met him at Romeo Salte, set her small gold-plated alarm clock—the kind that folded into a box, a hand-me-down from her mother—at the side of her table setting, and had a nice light lunch. A Greek salad.

"You're more beautiful than ever."

"Pass the pepper."

"You must marry me so that we can create a destiny that will bridge this life into the next one. Air travel is going to kill me one of these days. The turbulence on my last flight put me in chilling proximity to the deity."

"I want strawberries and cream for dessert, okay?"

"Of course."

"Thank you. With one of those little wafers they have over there at that table, see?" She giggled.

"Of course."

"Yummy."

She eyed the clock from time to time and had finished the strawberries and cream, two wafers, and her second cup of coffee when the alarm went off. She quickly depressed the stop button so as not to upset the staff and the other patrons of the restaurant.

"Thank you, darling, for a wonderful lunch," she said, getting up from her chair.

"You're not _seriously_ leaving?"

"But of course I am. A deal's a deal, right?"

"If you say so," he said, getting up from his own chair now.

He looked morose. But she knew their time had been perfect, and there was no use over-burdening a relationship that was ninety-nine percent fantasy with too prolonged an exposure to reality.

Anyway, she had to do the groceries.

All the Way Home
1959

1

ON A BEAUTIFUL FRIDAY MORNING IN AUGUST IN 1959, Carol and Walter decided to get married at City Hall. They had already gotten their license and blood tests, knowing they wanted to do it sometime soon. When they woke up that morning in Walter's Central Park West apartment, they decided today was as good a day as any. Aram and Lucy were with Bill in Paris for the summer. David and Jenny were with Gerry on Fire Island.

"But first," Carol said, standing in one of Walter's shirts, holding her coffee cup in the middle of the sunny room and smiling, "I want to buy a pretty dress at Jax. Korby there will know just the right thing."

"All right," Walter answered, seated on the edge of the bed in his blue robe, studying a racing form. "Let me get cleaned up here. And then I'll meet you at Ninety-third Street."

"Oh, Walter, are you sure you're not making a big mistake, darling? I know I'm the worst wife in the world. I've *proven* that."

Walter got up and walked over and put his arms around Carol. He kissed her on the nose.

She was outside Jax, near the corner of Fifty-seventh Street and Fifth, when Korby arrived to open it. Together they picked out a beige silk dress with a peach-colored rose pattern. It was just what she'd wanted.

She found Walter, now dressed in gray flannels with a sports jacket, a white shirt and a red tie, sitting at the marble table as she opened the door to the Ninety-third Street apartment. He had his racing form and a pencil.

"Oh, you're already here. You look divine, darling. What do you think?" Carol said from the center of the room.

"Oh, very nice," Walter said, looking up at her in the new dress. "*Very* nice, sweetheart."

Carol started making calls: Arnold, their lawyer; Lillian Ross, their writer friend; her sister, Elinor; and Walter's brother, Henry. Except for Henry, who agreed to meet them at City Hall at 2:00 that afternoon, everyone seemed to be out for the moment. She left messages with everyone's service.

She stood abstractedly at the front windows watching the Friday morning Madison Avenue traffic at the corner. The yellow cabs were like a herd of bright machines. She let her eyes dream for a moment.

When the telephone on the dark wood counter between the kitchenette and the living room rang, she all but leaped to answer it.

"Hello."

"I must see you immediately."

"Who is this?"

"Saroyan, it's Charles Dickens. Who do you *think* it is?"

"Oh, Ken . . . how are you?"

"I said I must see you immediately."

"That's not possible."

"Why not?"

"Because Walter Matthau and I are getting married today."

There was no immediate response. Suddenly all she could hear seemed to be shifting particles of dust in the circuit between them. It went on to the point when she was about to ask if he was still there.

"Congratulations!" he said then, very loudly, in a very proper English voice, and hung up.

Walter had bought her a ring at the five and ten to tide

them over until he could afford to buy her a real wedding ring. They got married that afternoon. Everyone she had phoned was there.

A week later, on the phone, she told Gloria about it. She hadn't invited her because she knew she and Sidney had been leaving for their house in Greenwich for the weekend. Anyway, from the beginning of her relationship with Walter, she had sensed that Gloria disapproved. Apparently, he wasn't quite chic enough or famous enough for her.

"Oh, but you *didn't*," Gloria said.

"Yes, darling, I did."

"Oh, but darling, you *didn't!*" Gloria insisted, her voice getting higher.

"Yes, Gloria, I *did*," Carol answered, getting flustered.

"Oh my God. Carol, you *know* you wouldn't have done this if I hadn't gone away for the weekend."

Well, you won a few and you lost a few, right?

"Oh, but darling, *why* did you do it?" Gloria pressed on.

Carol took a deep breath.

"Because I like to go to bed with him," she told her boldly.

Then Truman Capote called a few nights later and responded to the news by giggling.

"You're so inno-cent," he said.

"What do you mean, Truman?"

"Honey, you're just the most inno-cent little thing in this whole big city. *Nobody* does what you just did anymore."

"What did I do, darling?"

"You married for love, you crazy thing. I think it's the sweetest thing I ever heard of."

2

THE FOLLOWING SUMMER THEY MOVED FROM 53 EAST Ninety-third Street to a three-bedroom apartment on the twelfth floor at 451 West End Avenue that cost twenty dollars a month less.

Gloria and Sidney gave a garden party at "Faraway House," as they called their home in Greenwich. Everybody sat around the pool. And Gloria had everything so done up; it was like a fairy tale. Each little table with its Porthault tablecloth and a bouquet of flowers, and the wood-block cutting board, and all the fantastic food. It was a perfect, warm, fall afternoon.

The usual gang was there: Jack Warden, E. G. Marshall, the Avedons, Adolph and Phyllis Green, along with a few of the society crowd like Judy Peabody and the Eberstadts. It was funny, though, because Gloria really didn't give parties to see her friends, so much as to allow her friends to see *her*. Here she was, and beautiful; and the house was beautiful; and the servants were beautiful; and the food was beautiful; and— well, that was just who she was and, of course, she could be so terribly sweet, too. Or was Carol seeing everything with a little too much perspective lately? In any case, there was Gloria's notable coolness to Walter—before and *since* their marriage.

Then Walter, who felt understandably less than completely comfortable, sat down on the edge of a glass-topped table. Suddenly it broke, and he was hurt. He was bleeding.

Sidney took over immediately and got him into their car and drove with them to their doctor down the road. Walter was bleeding in the leg.

The doctor examined the cut in his office beside his house. It was a close call—it was high up on the leg—but Walter was okay. The doctor cleaned and bandaged the cut; and then they drove back to the party. They would, of course, go home now.

As she was getting her and Walter's things together while Walter waited in the car—Sidney had graciously insisted that their driver drive them home—she came across Gloria, three sheets to the wind.

"Oh, darling, is Walter all right?"

"Oh, yes, sweetheart, he's okay," she answered briskly. She didn't have time for an encounter.

"I mean *really* all right?"

Now she was going to be concerned; was that it? Now, when Carol only wanted to get Walter home.

"Oh, yes, he's fine."

"But I mean *really*, darling?"

Couldn't she see this just wasn't the *time* for this unprecedented display of sympathy? If, in fact, that was really what she had in mind.

"Yes, he's fine, Gloria."

"But darling, is he really, *really* all right?"

That she was stark, raving mad was another possibility. Carol took a deep breath.

"Yes, Gloria, he's really, really, *really* all right; and you're really, really, *really* crazy."

It seemed to dawn on her then that she had crossed a line. Well, *good*. She was so tired of tip-toeing around the delicate sensibilities of this insane millionairess who was so thoughtless about *other* people's feelings. Yes, she could also be very sweet, but it was just too impossible. Really just impossible.

3

Without making a conscious decision about it, Carol didn't phone Gloria for weeks, which then stretched into months. Then one night she got a call from Sidney Lumet, and they ended up having a long, rambling, easy-natured talk. Yet underneath it, she sensed there was some tension now between Gloria and him, although she steered the conversation away from any particulars. She just wanted to keep clear of Gloria for the time being.

That winter Walter opened as the lead in Harry Kurnitz's *Once More With Feeling*, which turned out to be a hit. Maybe because he knew he would be working steadily for a while, he began talking about their having a baby. Here she was, just getting out from under with Aram and Lucy—they were just beginning to start lives of their own—and it came as such a relief to her. She knew she hadn't done all she should have done for them. But she also knew she had done very nearly all that she could. A family just hadn't been in the cards for them, or for her.

Then one Sunday afternoon in their bedroom at 451, she fell asleep and had one of those peculiarly vivid dreams that seem to occur in the daylight hours. She dreamed she was lying on the bed she was, in fact, lying on—with the big television on wheels in the corner. But on her left, beside her on the bed, was a little bundle. Then she looked into the bundle, and there was this dream baby: the most perfect baby she'd ever seen, filled with love, and smiling. She was overwhelmed with happiness. Then she woke up.

· · ·

During the summer of 1962, in the fifth month of her pregnancy, she went with Walter to Greece where he played the part of a gangster in a movie called *Island of Love*. It was shot mostly on the island of Hydra.

At a break in Walter's shooting schedule, they went to Rome and stayed with Rosheen for two nights. Her mother looked beautiful—Walter said they looked like sisters together—and she had a big, cheerful apartment overlooking the Roman Forum. She gave a party for them and wore a decolletage that made everyone a little delirious, but she was darling to Walter and her. It was so good to see her somewhere, at last, with friends and a life of her own.

Then, after the picture was finished, they spent a few days with Oona and Charlie in Vevey, at the big house with its long, rolling lawn in the back that was so much like the house they'd had all those years ago on Summit Drive in Hollywood. And now they had *eight* children. Charlie had apparently stopped being embarrassed. For some reason, Walter went crazy for the food—she had never seen him eat so heartily— and Charlie, who met Walter for the first time on this visit, delighted in his appetite.

"I like the way that man takes his food," he told them all at the table. And to Walter: "You give me back my faith in life—watching you eat." And: "I know you want more of this corn, Walter. Here now, have more of this corn."

Inevitably, Carol and Oona sat up one night in the library-den off the big living room long after their husbands and the rest of the household had gone to sleep. They checked in, of course, on their perennial dilemma. Jimmy Michaelson and Wally Cosgrove were, they decided now, two boys who had played an important, top-secret role in preparing for America's future entry into the Second World War.

"Darling," Carol said, "it was mean of them not to tell us they were in espionage, wasn't it? After all, who could we have told?"

"Cholly Knickerbocker?"

"Who, by the way," Carol interjected in her more straight-forward tone, "I think *really was* a spy. Do you know what I mean? Think about it a minute, darling. Wouldn't that explain a lot of things? I may be wrong, but do me a favor and think about it."

"How's Gloria?" Oona asked her.

"Impossible. I'm not speaking to her and I had a terrible fight about her with Walter. Do you know what he accused me of—after all these years we've been friends? The three of us really like sisters, you and me and her. Do you know what he had the nerve to say to me?"

"What, darling?"

"He said, 'The only reason you've ever been interested in her is because her name is Gloria Vanderbilt.' Can you imagine saying that to me about Gloria?"

Oona, curled up at one end of the sofa with a plaid blanket around her, shrugged at Carol at the other end of the sofa, with another plaid blanket around her.

"Well," she deadpanned, "that's the only reason *I've* ever been interested in her."

Carol started laughing. That was Oona's marvelous, side-wise sense of humor. *She* had taken to Walter immediately, of course. But then, she was the only one of the three of them who had gotten marriage down on the first try.

4

LATE THAT SUMMER, CAROL AND WALTER RETURNED TO New York for just a few weeks before they would be going to Paris for him to make *Charade*. Carol was now in her seventh month, and she found herself preoccupied with little design touches in the baby's room as the big event drew closer. Ordinarily, she would have phoned Gloria immediately with all the details of her trip, the Chaplins, etc. It felt strange not to, and at the same time she'd heard rumors, even in Europe, that her marriage with Sidney was on the rocks.

Then one night Sidney called and they had another long talk. He was very down—really, she could hear, breaking up inside about the way things were going with Gloria. It was such a contrast to hear him in this state—so unlike his usual crisp and kinetic style. He really seemed to be, quite naturally, the Hollywood idea of the "director"—always hugging everybody and calling them "baby" and "sweetheart." And yet there was something genuinely sweet and generous in the way he did it. He told her he and Gloria had virtually separated— with Sidney now at Gracie Square in the city; and Gloria and the boys, Stan and Chris Stokowski, at Faraway House in Greenwich.

"But I gotta get outta here," Sidney told her. "The apartment's just us—everywhere I look. I'll tell ya, babe, it's getting to me."

"Yes, you should, Sidney. Get out of there. Get a new apartment. It'll be like breathing fresh air."

"Well, I wish it were that easy to *find* a place. But I've got to . . . I'll tell ya, just to look around here, you know, is like replaying a million little scenes . . ."

"Listen, darling, Walter and I are about to go back to Europe. He's doing a movie in Paris. The only one here is Helmi, you know, our housekeeper. Why don't you come and stay here? I'll send you the keys."

"You'd do that?"

"Of course. I'll send you the keys tomorrow."

"Honest to God?"

"I'm putting the keys in an envelope right now."

"Baby, sweetheart—you'd really do that for me?"

"Sidney, you're a friend. Of course I'll do it."

She mailed him the keys the next day with a note to tell

him when they'd be out of the apartment and when they'd be back. She felt awful for him, of course. How could you not? And for Gloria, too. Now that Carol was married to Walter, she had a sort of convert's sense of disappointment when anyone's marriage went bad. And here was poor Gloria at the end of her third. At the same time, it was sort of amazing the way men seemed to carry a torch for her even after she had decided she was done with them.

5

As IT TURNED OUT, CAROL CAME BACK BY HERSELF A FEW days early. She had gotten a hint of the onset of labor and she didn't want to take any chances on a French delivery. There was no sign of Sidney in the apartment, no sign that he'd even been there. But she barely had time to look. By the time Walter got back, she was in Doctors Hospital, where she'd had Aram nearly twenty years before.

It had been during those years, so long ago now, that she and Gloria, both young mothers in New York, had read a book called _The Prodigal Women_ by Nancy Hale. In the book the writer had talked about the experience of childbirth, and how as the baby was born a woman felt as though she were at the very center of the universe. She and Gloria agreed that Nancy Hale was a good writer.

"But, darling," she remembered Gloria saying to her one afternoon in her studio, "_I_ didn't feel like the center of the universe when _I_ had a baby, did you?"

That was Gloria's great gift, in a way—to go with her own experience and instinct. It was, she supposed, what she missed about her most. She, on the other hand, had sat there, before

Gloria said anything, wondering why *she* hadn't felt that she was the center of the universe. Maybe she just wasn't prodigal enough?

But there was something different about *this* baby. Well, there had been the dream, the sweet bundle by her side on her bed. That had been the beginning. Then there were the days of her pregnancy, the travel with Walter, a sense that their life together was opening and growing, even as the life inside her was growing.

Then, on December 10, 1962, she gave birth to a baby boy they named Charlie—after Daddy. And because it was such a lovely name. "Bonnie Prince Charlie" was a name that used to run through her mind when she was a child. Bonnie Prince Charlie must have been the sweetest baby. And he was.

Walter arrived in her hospital room with a coat he had bought her at Pierre Cardin and a little suitcase filled with perfume—both from Paris. He looked around the room, filled with flowers, smiling.

"You're more beautiful than these flowers," he said to her. She figured maybe she'd made it to the center of the universe.

6

AFTER SHE'D BEEN HOME FROM THE HOSPITAL FOR A WEEK or so, Carol remembered to ask Helmi if Mr. Lumet had used the apartment while she and Walter were in Paris. Helmi told her that he hadn't. She needed her keys back now, and one afternoon she phoned Sidney.

Everything had changed. He'd found a wonderful apartment, and had a wonderful new romance—with Gail Jones, Lena Horne's daughter.

"Oh, I'm so happy for you, Sidney. Really, darling, you deserve it, all of it. Listen, though, you've got to do me one big favor."

"You name it, sweetheart."

"Will you mail me back the apartment keys?"

"Oh, my God. Baby, do you know I'm sitting here staring at them. I don't know what I've been thinking. They're already in the envelope, babe."

"Oh, darling, that's fine. Thank you."

"Thank *you*."

But the keys never arrived, and, about three weeks later, she called him again, this time at his new apartment.

"Darling, I'm so sorry to bother you. I know it must have just slipped your mind..."

"The keys! You mean I didn't? No, I *know* I didn't, because you want to know something: I've got them right here. They're in the envelope ready to go. You'll have them tomorrow. I'm going to mail them as soon as I hang up. I'm sorry, sweetheart."

"Oh, Sidney, please. I know you've got a lot on your mind, darling."

But still the keys didn't come back. In the end, Carol decided to let it go. After all, calling twice was about as far as she could take it. She didn't want to become a pest just when Sidney was putting his life together again.

7

HE FOLLOWING FALL CAROL AND WALTER RECEIVED AN invitation to Sidney and Gail's wedding. Then, the day before the wedding, President Kennedy was shot. It was as if they—and everybody else, the whole country, really—had had the wind knocked out of them. They spent the following day, the day they had planned to attend the wedding, sitting on the floor of the living room, watching television, as the horror deepened.

Somehow Gloria got word that Carol hadn't attended the wedding, and it apparently had a special meaning to her.

"There's a letter for you from Gloria, pussycat," Walter told her one afternoon at the kitchen table just after the mail arrived. He handed her a thick envelope with Gloria's blue seal on the back. Five minutes later, Carol looked up into the white room with tears in her eyes. Walter put down his coffee mug.

"What's the matter?"

"Nothing," she said in a voice deepened with emotion, "but this is so sweet of her..."

The letter was the first communication between them in what she now realized, with amazement, was a couple of years—since Walter's accident at the house in Greenwich—and in it Gloria reaffirmed her love for Carol. My God, she thought, tears standing in her eyes, who in the world would ever care about me this much?

Well, she had to phone her now. She used the telephone in the bedroom.

"Darling, can you come right over?" Gloria asked.

"You mean right now?"

"Yes, just get in a cab and come over; there's so much I have to tell you."

An hour later, she took a taxi across the park—now the dark brown November colors—to 79th Street, and over to Gracie Square. When she got inside the penthouse—seeing the big black-and-white checkerboard squares on the foyer floor, she realized she'd *missed* them—Gloria introduced her to Wyatt Cooper, whom in fact she had met before. She and Walter had spent several evenings together with him and Leueen MacGrath, the actress, when they were seeing each other. He was an actor and a writer, a Southerner with lots of wry stories of his family, who had a handsome, almost cherubic, face and bearing and manner. He and Gloria looked marvelous together, as though they had each discovered their perfect weight, somehow, as a couple.

"Darling," Gloria told her almost before she'd gotten her coat off, "we're in love and we're going to get married. And do you want to know the funniest thing?"

"What?"

"Wyatt knows your mother. They knew each other in Rome."

"Oh, my God," Carol said, not certain what the proper response might be.

"Yes," Wyatt answered immediately and generously, "I know Rosheen. I think she's a wonderful woman."

Was it possible the world was really only about five miles square, most of it in New York, and the rest was done with mirrors?

They had tea in the den together. The day gradually faded at the window. They had come to terms again. Then Gloria told her a story.

"You know, darling, only one thing you did really hurt me. And then I figured it out, so it didn't anymore."

"What?" She really should be getting back across town. It was night outside now.

"It was while Sidney was staying here in the apartment and I was with the boys at Faraway House. Sometimes he would go away on business and I'd come in for a day or two. Well, I'd leave everything as he had it. I didn't want to touch or get back into his life again in any way, you know?"

"Of course," Carol nodded.

"There was really, in the entire apartment, just one drawer I opened. It was where I kept my nightgowns. And one night I opened it and there was your letter to Sidney with the keys Scotch-taped to it—the keys to your apartment. And that," Gloria finished with a laugh full of other resonances, "that, I must say, did hurt. It really did."

"Oh, but darling..."

"But wait a minute, darling," Gloria answered urgently,

"because then I thought about it. And I realized it wasn't you—it was Sidney. I mean he knew that that was the one drawer I'd open. And he *put* the letter there, so I'd *see* it. You know, in other words, 'This is what your best friend thinks of you.'"

"Oh, but you know it had nothing to do with you. He just sounded so..."

"Don't even talk about it, darling," Gloria said, lifting her hands. "No, really. Don't. You don't need to. That was just Sidney."

In the taxi home, she remembered Sidney's shattered mood when they'd talked before she sent him the keys. What he'd done certainly *had* been a little diabolical. Then she remembered the pain in his voice. She herself had a dim memory of what you could do when you were in pain like that.

A month or so later, Rosheen called from Rome. They chatted about Daddy and details of Walter's schedule, and then she remembered Gloria and Wyatt and told her mother Gloria was going to marry someone she knew, Wyatt Cooper.

Suddenly, the line was quiet for a moment, a very uncharacteristic intercontinental extravagance on Rosheen's part.

"Yes, I know Wyatt Cooper," her mother said then, in an accent that was suddenly very, very English, "and all I can tell you is that Gloria is going to be a very happy woman."

8

By the mid-sixties, Walter had become an established Hollywood movie star. After his big hit with Jack Lemmon, *The Odd Couple*, in which he repeated the role he had created on Broadway, he had starred in *Cactus Flower* with Ingrid Bergman and Goldie Hawn. He'd also made *Hello Dolly* with Barbra Streisand. At the end of the sixties, he and Carol moved to the West Coast. By this time, too, he had even survived a film that had been panned by the critics, although his own performance in the film had escaped the attacks.

"Oh, my God," he told Carol as they read a stack of bad reviews one sunny afternoon at the kitchen table at their new home in Pacific Palisades, "now I'm going to have to be nice to everybody again."

They laughed. In the end, it turned out, they needn't have been so worried. It was funny being a movie star, and being a movie star's wife.

It was at a party one night at "Swifty" and Mary Lazar's that she saw Ken Tynan again. He made a point of coming across the room to where she was standing.

"Saroyan," he said, looming over her, holding a drink, "I have just one thing to say to you. Never before—never again. You were the one. And you will always be that one..."

For a moment or two, she was laughing—flattered, as of course she always had been. But it went on and on, and she grew more and more uneasy. Then something broke.

"Ken," her own voice almost surprised her, "don't you talk to me that way!"

Here she was, suddenly and decisively calling a halt to

another sustained romantic onslaught. For at that moment it seemed clear that there was something terribly wrong with his speaking to her in that way with Walter, her husband, standing on the other side of the room. She looked up at him sharply.

"Don't make a mistake about Walter and me," she told him. "Don't get the idea we're in the same league as the other couples in this room. We're not together because we once were together. We're not together because I do his laundry. I'm with him because I'm deeply, deeply in love with him, and I don't ever want you to speak like that to me again. Do you understand?"

Ken seemed visibly to flinch. He made a noise as if swiftly sucking in air. He looked at her only a moment longer. Then he turned and vanished from her life into the Hollywood party.

PART THREE

*W*hat makes us free is the knowledge who we were, what we have become; where we were, wherein we have been thrown; whereto we speed, wherefrom we are redeemed; what is birth and what rebirth.

—*Valentinus, Roman*

The View at the Plaza
1972

1

CHARLIE SMILED INSIDE THE LIMOUSINE'S MUFFLED SUN-light and moved toward the door. Oona reached in after him, but he waved her away.

"I'm not *that* old, am I?"

"Of course not, darling."

Such a radiant pink he was—but it had to be a strain, all this. Well, it was on *her*—some kind of blank terror under it all, too. He didn't feel *that*, she knew. No, it was the old New York that would scare her like this. The famous Debutante-of-the-year-Stork-Club-Oona-O'Neill New York that would drive her up...

The doorman, with that gray-and-thin-red-striped uniform still—some crazy fascination in that once upon a time—reached in after Charlie.

"No, no, I don't *need* any help, damn it!"

And she smiled at the poor young man in the chilly April sunlight, turning away from Charlie, who was ready, possibly, to strangle the young man, cancel their reservations, and return to Vevey for a slow afternoon tennis game with her.

Pit...pat, pit...pat, pit...pat. Like a funny kind of loving talk with the ball and rackets. She and Charlie in the green and quiet, and maybe Christopher watching from the sideline, the little boy and his father so close. Charlie with all his life inside, eighty-three years old and pink as a baby, and Christopher, just at the beginning of it all: natural magnets, she supposed.

And then there he was beside her on the sidewalk—re-splendent presence in the adorable chocolate suit he hated. A couple of photographers darting around, and about two hundred people, well-wishers, fans, cordoned off on either side of the entrance with those official sawhorses they used, plus a dozen or so police. Charlie waved now and blew a kiss to each side, and a cheer went up. But this would be it. No press conference. Why bring up a lot of bad feelings on either side? Stick to the honors being given him for his art. And then too, as he'd told a young woman at a dinner party that winter: "My dear, I've had a series of small strokes and I don't remember a single thing about anything."

And it was the truth—at least at times. Yet happy as a baby—almost—maybe. But that was his magic from the be-ginning, after all, wasn't it? Fiddling with the cane, that crazy walk, twirling with everything (including dying now, too? No, don't even think it)—mysterioso, as Bill Saroyan used to say, and laugh like the happiest man in the world.

She had to phone Carol. *That* would be fun. Girl talk while Charlie napped. She took his arm and they went up the steps, through the door, and into the lobby, the wood-paneled, red-carpeted Plaza, buzzing with its human traffic, all the after-noon's priorities. A bellboy suddenly to their right.

"Mr. and Mrs. Chaplin, right this way, please!"

They had the elevator to themselves, the bald smiling el-evator man standing forward and erect in that uniform again. The creases so sharp, the ruler of his little kingdom: all the important passengers he carried up and down, up and down.

"Watch your step, please," he said crisply, opening the doors.

And he'd made a perfect landing.

2

THEN THE BIG AIRY ROOMS—WHITE WITH RED TRIM. MAR-velous. Charlie on a chair, his jacket off, white shirt opened at the collar, red suspenders, breathing with pleasure.

"Darling, it's so pretty!"

"It is, isn't it, sweet?"

She glanced a kiss over his cheek—fresh, pink, and cold, like some heavy flower. Touched his thick, soft hand.

"It's spring, Charlie. Central Park looks lovely."

"Cold, though. But I can see you wish we'd never left."

Huh. "Never!"

He laughed quietly, mirth circulating through him.

"What're all those roses?" he asked.

"Oh, Gloria and Wyatt. So darling. I must call her about tonight. Are you up to it?"

"Yes, but not to talk, only to look. I like looking, though. My life's going back to the silents."

"Not with me around."

She had made herself a martini at their little dark wood bar, letting Central Park catch her eye again. The little green things. Another Manhattan April.

"Darling, a nap?"

"Oh, yes. Thank you. Good."

He'd forgotten. He got up and she walked with him into the master bedroom, pulled the shades down while he re-moved his shoes and lay down. The room went gradually dark gray, the blue vibrancy only peeking at the edges of the shades. She sat down beside him for a moment, pulling the plaid blanket at the foot of the bed up over him.

"Rest, darling."

"All right, sweet. Then we'll..."

Funny smile.

"What, Charlie?" She smiled.

"Do the town," he whispered, his eyes closed now.

She sat for a moment or two while his breathing grew slower and denser. He liked her by him when he went off.

3

WELL NOW, THE PLAZA. FROM THE LIVING ROOM WINdow, she gazed down at the horses and buggies, one of those sort of somnolent, sunny New York afternoons. A couple walks by. One of the buggy drivers says something to them but they keep going as the horse's tail sweeps up almost in slow motion in back.

Her heyday. Enough to make her father hate her. Debutante of the Year at the Stork Club. Interviewed for her opinion on the war. Sense enough to balk at that one. Possible headline: OONA HATES WAR. Who knows, it might have turned the whole thing around. Especially if she could have gotten Carol and Gloria in a consensus: BIG THREE ADAMANT: FIGHTING MUST STOP. She sat down beside the phone with her rose print address book from Carol—to give Gloria a call. But she found herself giving the receptionist Carol's number in Pacific Palisades. She got Mary, the cook.

"Oh, it's you, Mrs. Chaplin. Yeah, she's here for *you*."

Then a pause. Then Carol's breathless whisper.

"Hello."

Like the wind in the trees. *Wuthering Heights*. How many times—eleven? twelve?—at that Thirty-sixth Street Trans

Lux with the little man in a black suit who let them in cheaper if they paid him and not the ticket seller in the booth.

"Hi, we're at the Plaza."

"Oh, darling, welcome home!"

"Uh—I've been looking at Central Park and remembering Jimmy Michaelson and Wally Cosgrove. Charlie's asleep."

"Isn't New York beautiful, Oona?"

"Oh, it is, darling. But—oh, I suppose I should just enjoy it."

"But do me one favor."

"What?"

She could hear a helicopter outside over the city.

"Don't enjoy it too much. Because my party has to be the *best*, okay?"

"Of course, sweetheart."

"Have you talked with her? She's so excited."

"I was about to, but I gave your number instead."

"Oh, she's pulling out her stops and I'm pulling out mine and the world is never going to be the same."

"What're you eating?"

"One of Mary's BLTs."

"Umm."

"We'll have 'em when you get here. Oh, darling, I can't wait. Is Charlie okay?"

"Divine, darling."

"It's not too much for him?"

"Oh, no. He's thrilled."

The little chat with Carol was like a quick decompression, back to basics, Carol and the BLTs. Possible rock group? Even when Bill was making her turn cartwheels, she'd had that down-to-earth instinct. Pass the ketchup. Which was wisdom, damn it, even if everybody else thought it was something (somebody) else.

She found her martini by the bar and stood another moment

abstractedly before the Central Park South panorama, hazy with the traffic noises and that New York roar under it all. Carol and her walking home in their bobby socks and saddle shoes with their schoolbooks in front of them. Now it was Peter . . . what's his name? . . . Frampton. Then it was Artie Shaw. And her father would hate-hate-hate her. The poor, sad, serious man. Long gone now.

In the limousine that evening, they turned up Madison Avenue—such silvers and blacks, the little glints of light everywhere on it. Make mine Manhattan, at least tonight. She wore her yellow gown with a white velvet stole (one of Charlie's favorites of her dinner outfits). And at East Sixty-seventh Street, as they got out—Gloria. That radiant smile of her lifetime. My God, how beautiful she looked. Wyatt must be good for her. And he too, looking so young. A couple of kids or something. Hadn't she figured out that nobody in love gets older because love is bigger than time? Prove it.

Oh my God. Their little boys.

"And this is Carter. And Anderson."

"Hello, hello."

"Welcome, Mrs. Chaplin."

"Oh, please. *Oona.*"

They were combinations, the older one with a bit of Gloria's father's features. Old Reggie, whom none of them had ever seen. (Including Gloria.) Charlie shook hands with both the little boys. Gloria looking so sleek in a black sheath dress. And her scent; was it Joy?

"Darling, it's so good to see you."

"Oh, Oona. Come in, darling. I've got a spot all ready for Charlie so he won't have to stand all night."

"Oh, good."

Lillian Gish, wasn't it, by the hors d'oeuvre table? And Senator Javits. Gloria's house—those fabrics, everything so lush and sweet-smelling and carefully chosen. Candles everywhere. Rigaud. Their vanguard. Carol's and hers. The bright, flashing siren of their lives. In Hollywood marrying Pat di Cicco before you could say School Graduation, and Carol and Oona clambering after her. They knew a good thing when they saw one. "We'll be just like her." And they were, at least until Charlie came along.

Oh good, Wyatt sat him down by the fire. Charlie's television now. They'd been on the news getting off the plane, Charlie waving, making news in America again, so many years after sneaking out of New York so he wouldn't be served with that subpoena. An ex-employee of United Artists—the corporation Charlie had founded with Douglas Fairbanks and Mary Pickford to stop the giant merger of all the studios planned by strictly business interests at the beginning of the first World War—was suing the company just then for so many millions. Charlie Schwartz, Charlie's lawyer, told him it was nothing but a nuisance action, but all the same advised him to lie low because if he was served a summons, it could mean he'd be called back from their vacation. Dick Avedon's photograph of him, taken the afternoon just before their getaway: like Pan, with his fingers the horns, eyes dancing. Goodbye.

They spent the evening sitting together, greeting everyone. Just one slip: Charlie mistakenly raising his hand to shake hands with the hors d'oeuvre tray. It was quite lovely.

5

THEN HOME AGAIN, THANK GOD, BY ELEVEN. CHARLIE
and she both in bed and she could hear him sleeping now.
She touched his foot with her foot. Always so warm, while
her own still had a chill in it. Charlie's life so warm to her.
He made America warm up again.

Her stepmother, Carlotta, that summer of 1941 at her father's
Carmel estate, Tao House: "My dear, have you considered
nursing?"

"No, Carlotta, I want to be a movie star. I wouldn't be a
good nurse."

The poor witch could have croaked. Though she still hadn't.
In some nursing home somewhere, probably had the entire
staff under lock and key. The Godfather. Don Corleone off
the deep end. And her poor father must have needed...

His mother, of course.

Her mother, Agnes, struggling to write, to love, to live—after
he went off with his maternal mood indigo, Carlotta Monterey,
a kind of human peninsula. Wraparound. An early earthwork
for her daddy's mother-starved soul. Only she had to make
sure he forgot his own children. Poor Shane—Oona must call
him in New Jersey.

But that summer she'd seen her father at Tao House they'd
gotten along so. She was sixteen, and it turned out to be the
last time she saw him, and she could count the times before
on her fingers. That was what made it so hard.

"You'll be a grand woman," he said with that shy, glancing-away light in his eyes, as shy as she was with him. "Stay away from Hollywood."

Fat chance. Did God make little green apples? Is your daughter Oona *the* movie-crazy American girl? But hadn't it been the best, better-than-the-best thing in the world for her to do?

Manhattan below. Manhattan above. Only in Manhattan. Like sleeping under the trees in Bermuda when she was little. Shane king of the fort.

"I'm king!"

"No, I want to be king!"

"You can't be king. You're a girl, stupid!"

"I can too."

True grit—at least next to Shane's dreamer mold. Yes I can. A bit of Sammy Davis, Jr., in her—but enough? Not until Charlie came along.

Big avenues below, lights on Broadway. She should wake up Charlie, get Bill and Carol, and go pub crawling—like old times.

Well, Bill would have to fly in from Fresno, or that walk-up in Paris. What had happened with him? And Aram and Lucy? Michael had seen Aram in London and he'd been smoking marijuana, but that was the sixties. Carol said he'd gotten married, and Lucy was somewhere in New York. Acting? Little Lucy, my God.

She got up and walked in her nightgown in the dark to the window. Another look. Was it midnight? Charlie turned in bed. The horses and buggies looked the way they'd looked when she was a girl, living at Carol's when she wasn't downtown with her mother.

Divine midnight light at the Plaza. All those debutante dances.

6

Birds twittering across the street in Central Park. The late-morning jitters. Room service. Charlie dressed, perusing the *Times* at the table, a front-page story about their arrival yesterday and the Lincoln Center do tonight, under a headline about Mr. Nixon considering resuming the bombing of North Vietnam.

"Let's take a walk, shall we?"

Well, *he* was chipper.

"Wonderful. I'll be just a minute."

She went into the bathroom.

"It's nice to be an old man," he said. "You get to be idle."

She came out of the bathroom and looked at him.

"Oh, but you're not."

He put the paper aside.

"I dreamed about Hollywood last night. It's a wonder I'm still alive."

"That bad?"

"Exhausting. Fun, but exhausting!"

She wrinkled her eyes and made her voice louder.

"*How* much fun?"

"Oh, you were there, my dear. You were there."

"Good!"

She walked over and kissed him and he got up from the table, smiling.

Wearing topcoats, they left the suite together, rode the elevator to the lobby, went out the front entrance of the Plaza, and emerged, as anonymously as they had arrived anywhere in years, in midtown Manhattan.

"Let's walk downtown."

"Good."

When they got to Fifth Avenue, in the sunny cold, she felt an exhilarating lift. Suddenly part of the horde, the endless daytime stream, and nobody you knew. What was it exactly? Those long bus rides from Carol's downtown to Agnes's, when she could read Willa Cather or Thomas Wolfe and glance out at Fifth Avenue, and the other passengers around her were all so much warmth and reassurance.

They stood in a crowd at the Fifty-seventh Street intersection, the crosswalk of the world, waiting for the light to change.

"I brought my sunglasses. Did you bring yours?"

She rummaged in her Hermès bag. "Yes, they're right here."

"Good."

They both put their glasses on and walked now that the light was green and the sign said WALK. Everybody, now.

And maybe, out the bus window one of those afternoons, it was snowing. Even cozier. So the print in the book, with that voice of the prairie in it, that quiet, beautiful voice, mixed in with the weather's white light and the rhythm of the bus stopping and starting, people getting on and getting off, shaking the wet from themselves, as rosy and exhilarated as the prose in her book. A bus ride, reading. Like life: in and out, and around, and back inside again. You.

"Did you enjoy the party last night?" she asked him, passing Doubleday's.

"You know, I enjoyed it very much. They're a sweet couple."

"I don't think Gloria's ever been better."

"Well, Wyatt's *with* her. You sense that."

"Yes." As you are, dear, with me.

• • •

Joe Schenk it was who finally told her to see Charlie and forget what everybody else said. Uncle Joe, the head of Twentieth Century Fox, where Pat di Cicco was working as one of Joe's assistants. Joe said yes. And she was dying to meet Charlie Chaplin, of course, anyway. She owed that to Joe Schenk—going to read for the Irish girl in *Shadow and Substance*, a play he was considering adapting for the movies.

"Remember Uncle Joe?"

"Of course."

Suddenly she was giggling. They were going by Rockefeller Plaza. Atlas holding up the world. Up, up.

"What?" he turned to her. She held on to his arm and kept their pace.

"I just remembered the George Cinq story."

Joe Schenk couldn't speak a word of French but when he got into a cab in Paris, he'd say his name, Joe Schenk, and the driver would take him right to his hotel, the George V.

Charlie chuckled. Not a word spoken. Like Walter's joke about the prison where they tell jokes by number. Like marriage, too, she supposed. The good ones. And the bad?

Joe Schenk told her to go see Charlie, and she went. There he was—those blue eyes.

"*Hello!* Why, let me look at you. You mean your father's Eugene O'Neill?"

"Yes."

"Well, my dear; I was expecting more of a sepia impression, do you follow?"

He laughed and she laughed. Sepia impression—perfect. And there he was, fifty-two, looking thirty-two, possibly forty. So strong. The elegance of his energy. Like the films.

A dancer—in life, too.

She did the screen test, too, but by then it didn't matter. She was in love with Charlie and he wanted to marry her. She felt suddenly as though she was living a whole new life. She supposed she was really happy for the first time in her life.

And everybody told her she didn't know what she was getting into—the Joan Barry paternity suit, etc. Joan Barry and her knockers. The innocent minor. Please. By the time Charlie was cleared, they were already married. He had wanted to wait, for her sake, for the outcome of the trial, but she wanted to get married and forget about the trial. But obviously the outcome meant more to her than she'd thought because when she got the news that he was acquitted of the Mann Act charges, she fainted.

Now as they approached the Forty-second Street library, they turned around, and she caught the eye of a cabdriver idling his car at the corner.

"Perfect," Charlie said inside the little cave of the taxi as they headed uptown. He put his hand down over hers.

7

In their rooms again, Charlie went in for a nap. She sorted through five or six messages, including an incomprehensible one from Shane. She gave the operator the number, but there was no answer. She got up and walked to the view again. The light in New York as clear as some surgical operation platform. Please remove my past, and make it snappy. Daddy, Mommy, the Stork Club.

She should read the newspaper. But she couldn't. She sat down by the window, dreaming over Central Park. No complete thoughts as she let her eyes lose their focus for a moment. Then returned them to the particularities of daylight: the budding trees across the street. Only Geneva seemed comparably clear, but not quite so penetrating a light. New York light struck right into you.

She went to answer the telephone. The receptionist said it was a Mr. and Mrs. O'Neill downstairs. *Daddy and Carlotta? Send them up, they've arrived straight from hell.* But this must be Shane and Cathy, of course. What could she say? She'd meet them for tea downstairs? Charlie should sleep.

"Well, send them up."

She hung up and went to the mirror and smoothed her black Chanel suit. One of her nicest hit-and-run purchases in Paris one afternoon with Charlie waiting in the car. Always together. One man, one mind. His mind? But what if she were left behind?

8

SHE GOT UP AND WALKED TO THE DOOR AND OPENED IT and there were four people. Her mind careened but then her eyes met Shane's eyes, like a high place in a flood.

"Shane!"

"Oona!"

They hugged. And then Cathy and her.

"But this can't be..."

But it was. Ted and Kathleen. And they were as big as their parents. She hugged them too.

"Oh, but you're all so dressed up. You look wonderful. Come in!"

Her crazy brother in a suit and tie, Cathy so scrubbed and done up, and the grown-up children all so—wonderful looking. The afternoon light in little patches all over the room, the furniture, and this family.

"Sit down. Would you like something to drink? Some wine?"

"Great," Shane answered, surveying the living room. "We called, but I guess the message didn't get through." He sat down in a red leather armchair by the window just a little disconsolately: that old rhythm of his coming to the fore.

"Oh, no, it did. I've been expecting you. Charlie's just resting."

"It's tonight, right?"

"Yes, the Lincoln Center ceremony."

She set out two glasses at the bar. Now, someone needed to tell her a secret. How could they be so normal, as they say? After all, Shane had it bad, and Cathy managed to stick by him, just, through those years: the handsome dreamer who never in his life seemed to wake up.

Now suddenly here's Ted, as big as his dad, with—manners. Youth so lovely in that way, given some guidelines. The energy inside it, that bloom. Look at him. Leaning forward on the sofa next to his sister with his hands just so.

Their own household, hers and Charlie's—an absolute battlefield at times: Michael coming in the front door and Charlie punching him in the nose. Marijuana. Did Bill ever punch Aram?

She brought Shane and Cathy their glasses of wine. Cathy sipped hers. "Umm."

She could have died—for Michael and for Charlie. Yet what could be said? The sixties in Vevey, too.

"Charlie, really though! He's just trying to get out of the nest."

"He's had every advantage and he's spoiled rotten and I'll teach him if it's the last thing I do."

An old man winded in the sunny evening. Michael run off somewhere, hiding, the tender soul of their first son. But Charlie, in the end, had to be her priority.

"What would you like? Wine too?"

Ted and Kathleen thought about it a moment. There was a series of honks in the street.

"A Coke?" Ted said.

"Sure."

"I'd love one," said Kathleen.

"Ted," Cathy said from her chair beside them, "why don't you serve them and let Aunt Oona sit down."

"Oh, it's no trouble." But Ted was already there at the bar. "Well, they're in the little icebox then. Right. All right, thanks."

She sat down on the chair on the other side of the sofa opposite Cathy.

Charlie so sort of practical about it all, his savvy almost terrifying at times: figuring out how to reach Michael. But reaching too far. Michael still in tears when she found him, in his basement hideaway, with bloody Kleenexes in his bloody nose.

"I hate that son of a bitch, and I'll hate him for the rest of my life." His book, later, *I Couldn't Smoke the Grass on My Father's Lawn.*

"Michael, he's—" What could she say? *He's confused? He loves you? He's not always great with kids? Remember what he did with Aram when he was ten?*

"Oh, and please have some fruit," she said, putting her hand out to the hotel's big complimentary bowl on the black marble coffee table.

Kathleen smiled and took a plum.

They had Aram come out for two weeks to Vevey while Carol went to London for that voice-over job. The kids had been playing and Aram picked up Josephine and she wriggled out of his arms and fell onto the grass. She came into the house weeping. Charlie took one look and was ready to kill.

"What happened?"

"Aram dropped me." Stuttered out between her sobs, their six-year-old raving beauty. They'd been about to play tennis.

"Dropped you?"

Ted brought two Cokes in glasses back to the sofa, gave one of them to Kathleen, and sat down again, smiling. Then he took a peach.

"Yes. He dropped me."

"Charlie, they were playing—the way kids do . . ."

"I'll talk to him and find out."

"Please. Charlie. He's not a mean boy."

They looked into each other's eyes. Or was he? Charlie would find out.

He found Aram playing with Michael and Geraldine and called him aside. He walked with him into the woods, and announced to the ten-year-old boy that Josephine would probably die. He needed to know every detail of what had happened.

Let's get down to basics. Talk to a ten-year-old's mind as he would later talk to a nineteen-year-old son, Michael—with a punch in the nose. Except that the boy, Aram, grew ashen. Charlie suddenly knew he had made a stronger impression than was, strictly speaking, necessary. The flip side of genius. And they had to watch this ten-year-old contemplate himself as a possible murderer for a couple of days. A bit gruesome.

But now then, her brother, eyes darting around the appointments of the Plaza suite. A half smile, dentistry apparently intact. No wig, thank God. Just an honest, bald New Jersey-ite. Carol's telephone crush. And then Carol's astonishment in Nice when Oona brought her up to date.

"What about Shane, Oona?"

"Don't ask."

"Why? He always seemed so sweet on the phone."

"Oh, he is. But—well, the war was awful for him. He saw real horrors. And then he came home and got hooked on drugs."

"Oh my God. What's he like now?" Wide-eyed, one of those nights they sat up talking in the French provincial guest room, inky night outside.

"Don't ask."

"Really?"

"He looks like an egg. He's absolutely bald and has no teeth."

"No teeth?"

"It's the heroin."

"Oh my God."

But here he was now, a solid, respectable-looking New Jersey burgher in a tweed jacket and large businessmen's shoes. The teeth, in fact, looked better than they had when they were real.

"It's so good to see you all."

"Good to see you, Oona!" He smiled at her and got up and looked out the window, turned toward that vista, still resonant for him too?

"My God, Cathy, the children..."

"Well, it goes so quickly, doesn't it?"

"Oh, it does."

Indeed it does. The years filling in while she was away. Now to suddenly come face to face with it, all at once: like a color photograph that seems to contain just slightly more color than exists, this grown-up family.

A breeze went through the room and made the cover of *Vogue* on the coffee table stand suddenly vertical—then, slowly, let it return to its horizontal position.

"Are you parked?"

At the window, Shane turned to her.

"Parked?"

"I meant the car."

"Oh, we got a train in."

"Oh, yes. Of course."

She stood up.

"Let me look in on Charlie. He was napping."

"Oh." Cathy looked alarmed. "Please don't disturb him."

"Oh, no, I won't. He's fine."

9

SHE WENT THROUGH THE DOOR INTO THE DARKNESS OF the bedroom. She backed up against the door now, closing it quietly behind her, her eyes adjusting to the darkness. After a moment she could tell he was awake because she couldn't hear him breathing.

"Who's out there?" he said, sounding anxious.

"Darling, it's Shane and Cathy and two grown-up kids. It's..."

"What, sweet?"

He sat up; he was wearing his shirt and slacks under the blanket. He turned on his bed-table light. He looked so serene, rested. Suddenly she could feel tears glazing her eyes.

"My God, Charlie, they're grown up. And everybody's so dressed up."

She came and sat on the edge of the bed. He put his arm around her and kissed her temple.

"Now, don't go all mushy on me," he told her. "I'm eighty-three and I refuse to be swept into grief at time's passing. It won't do me a bit of good."

She started to laugh.

"That's better." He tickled her under her rib cage for a moment. She wriggled up, wiping her eyes, smiling. Then she raised the shades and light flooded the room so that the bed lamp's radiance disappeared.

"That's better now. Now bring the sons of bitches in for a visit, will you?"

"Charlie!"

"Oh, I'd love to see them. You know that."

"Really?"

"Go!"

10

SHE USHERED THE FAMILY INTO THE BEDROOM, AS IF OUT of the rain of her own hesitations, memories, awkwardness, impasses. Well, they sure as hell couldn't discuss their father's copyrights now, could they?

"When's the last time you saw Long Day's Journey into Night?"

"Me? Oh, I see it every day. Gorgeous piece of work, isn't it?"

So Charlie would bring it all back to some semblance of reality. They had dressed for *him*, after all.

"Oh, they've grown up," he said, surveying the family. "My God, that's Ted. You know how big you were the—well, let me see if I can remember."

"I was just born."

"That's right. You were just born. And who is this delicious creature?"

"Kathleen," said Kathleen with the sweetest smile.

"I've got an idea, if you'll go along with a very old Englishman..."

Kathleen smiled again.

"Don't you laugh at me!" Charlie had made himself suddenly wizened and grim, speaking in a gruff old voice. "I may be old but I've still got every last one of my marbles." Then in a sudden Cockney aside: "Course, there was only two to begin with. Little ones at that."

Everyone was laughing.

"Sit down, why don't you," he said, waving them all into chairs. "And what I was going to say is—if you'll indulge me, they have a very nice tea here, and we can get them to bring it up to us."

"Lovely," said Cathy, amidst the others' murmurs of pleasure.

Thank God for Charlie, right, gang? Not that Oona didn't want it that way, the way he did it for them just then, but only that, strictly speaking, on a day such as this and at this point in time, she simply *couldn't*.

11

HADN'T SHE AND SHANE BEEN LITTLE BETTER THAN ORphans, when you came right down to it? And then, with Carlotta holding his hand—forming the letters?—her father had actually disinherited them both, too. Well, by that time, he couldn't forgive her for *Charlie*—the paternity suit, the press making them out some father-daughter fixation. She was so upset by it all, she finally said something about it to Charlie, fifty-two that year she was eighteen.

"Oh, yes, I know," he said. "It's awful, isn't it? All that nonsense they print. But, after all"—and now he was looking into her eyes with the whole, marvelous being that he was—"what we have together, isn't it lovely?"

In other words, who really knew what they were? He himself an orphan of the London streets while she came out of a black Irish, shanty Irish struggle in the new world, with everybody going slightly cockeyed in the process. And there they were, suddenly, at the top of the world.

You don't say no to the best thing life ever gave anybody. When love comes along and the world is everything it was rumored to have been all your long, dim life, you don't fiddle around thinking. You don't get picky about birth dates and political positions and this and that and the other. You just

215

get very happy and hope it'll last forever.

And, of course, Shane was on drugs by then. So their father wrote them out of their inheritance, which is like writing them both, Shane and her, and himself too, right out of time. Into some netherworld of missed connections, the purgatory of no deeper continuity than this moment. Sort of the whole story of America, wasn't it?

You don't need anything when you're young, damn it. You need it when you see your own children grow up into themselves, like hers and like Shane's, here and now. Geraldine and Michael and Ted and Josephine and Kathleen and Victoria and...

And you can't even say anything about it, discuss it, with a man in his grave. It's irrevocable. She was, under it all, so *angry* at that crazy, haunted man who happened to have been her father.

12

THE CEREMONY AT LINCOLN CENTER WAS FOLLOWED BY a champagne gala with a thousand guests. Sitting together at a banquet table, Charlie raised his hand again and again, greeting one well-wisher after another. Suddenly it was Jackie Coogan standing there beside them, but Charlie acted as though he were just one more well-wisher while the poor man went on talking, waiting for a glimmer of recognition. She poked him.

"Darling, this is Jackie Coogan," she whispered into his ear.

But Charlie remained impassive while Coogan—no longer the delicate "kid" but a strapping, red-nosed, middle-aged man—went on talking. Was it possible Charlie had slipped out of his mind for a moment? It had been known to happen more frequently in the last year or so.

She poked him again as Coogan went on, now gazing forlornly into the middle distance, and whispered, "Charlie, it's Jackie Coogan, 'the kid,' darling."

Now he poked her back.

"Stop poking me," he whispered into her ear. "He wants residuals."

They arrived back at their rooms after one that evening, both of them equally exhausted. The rooms suddenly had a sort of forlorn, Edward Hopper quality. She fell asleep without even looking out the window again. The next day they checked out and took the plane to California. Charlie was going to receive an Academy Award for his lifetime of achievement in film.

PART FOUR

Remember my little granite pail?
The handle of it was blue.
Think what's got away in my life—
Was enough to carry me thru.

—Lorine Niedecker

The Last Fairy Tale
1972

1

HAVING COME WITH WALTER TO LUNCH WITH OONA AND Charlie at the Polo Lounge in the Beverly Hills Hotel, Carol for the first time could see the years on Charlie. He was sweet, as always, but vague and quiet.

"How do you feel about a party tomorrow, Charlie?" Walter asked him over dessert at their table at the far end of the L-shaped greenhouse of the restaurant. Walter knew how to come to the point. Charlie looked up and smiled.

"Yes," he said, beaming at Walter, and Carol exchanged a glance with Oona, who was smiling too. It was funny how Carol could never see the years on *her*. They hadn't seen each other since 1967, only a year or so after Walter's heart attack (they'd gone to Vevey after Walter finished making *Candy* in Rome), and yet it was as if she were sitting on the twin bed opposite hers in her bedroom at 420 Park Avenue, both of them still in school.

"Darling, it's so good to see you. Both of you—" she said, turning to Charlie as well. But he had his eyes on Walter, who was about to leave for the Academy Awards rehearsal.

"Do you feel like rehearsing, Charlie?" Walter asked him.

She knew he'd promised Howard Koch, who was producing the show, that he'd give it one last try, but Oona had all but pronounced it an impossibility on the phone that morning.

"He really is exhausted, darling. All the jet lag accumulates as you fly west, for some reason. You don't really feel it the other way."

"Oh, I know."

And she'd reported that back to Walter. But now Charlie looked vaguely tempted. He liked Walter so much he might have gone with him for an hour or so, maybe. But he looked quickly at Oona, and then back at Walter.

"I've got a very important nap coming up, Walter."

Walter's eyes smiled appreciatively, and he looked from Charlie over at her, and then at Oona.

"Okay, guys," he said, getting up from his chair. "No, I just meant you, Charlie. You're the other guy here. And okay, you two beautiful, adorable, *insanely sexy* ladies. Be seeing you in a little while."

And he leaned down to give Carol a kiss, and then, smiling, gave Oona one too.

"I told Mary we'd be eating at six, Poppy. Is that okay?" Carol asked, looking up at him in the room's diffused daylight.

Walter stood for a moment, considering.

"You told her six?"

"Yes, is that okay?"

"I don't know, sweetheart. I guess so. I hope it is because if it isn't Mary'll be angry," he said, turning to Charlie and Oona, his eyes smiling again.

"Oh, it's true. Mary's very tough," Carol said of their cook in a general explanation to the table at large. "Poppy and I have to be careful what we do."

"Very careful, that's right." Walter said with mock severity as he began to mosey toward the door. "Oh, yes. *Very* careful."

He stopped at a table to say hello to someone on his way out of the restaurant.

2

After lunch, Carol walked back with Oona and Charlie to their bungalow at the hotel. It was one of those warm but muggy days with a sky like white laundry that the sun could never quite break through. Inside their bungalow, after the little walk from the restaurant, Charlie suddenly seemed his old self again. Oona mentioned Truman Capote, who had helped him revise his autobiography, and suddenly Charlie was impersonating Truman.

"That'th not a thententh. It'th not a thententh, and it never *will be* a thententh."

Then, by way of punctuating this remark, he did a fast pirouette in the middle of the room's blue and white country-style decor.

"Oh my God, Charlie," Carol said, "Truman's never looked so wonderful!"

"Oh, he's fun," Charlie answered, flushed and smiling. "And not a bad editor at all."

"The best!" Carol pronounced authoritatively, tapping her knuckles on a teakwood table holding a lamp with a flower print shade. She recognized a certain nervousness in her own gesture. Her writing career—close to twenty years now in hiatus.

"Well, it's time for me to be unconscious."

"Oh, yes," Oona said. "Do have a nap, darling."

Carol walked to Charlie and hugged him goodbye.

"Ooh, Charlie, I hope we're going to see you tomorrow."

"Oh yes, sweetheart."

He went into the bedroom, closing the door and leaving Carol and Oona in the living room.

"Your clothes aren't in there, are they?" Carol asked Oona with sudden urgency a moment after the door had shut.

"Oh no, darling, they're all in the trunk here," she said, pointing out an upright portable closet beside a blue and white upholstered chair with a pattern of jonquils on it.

"Oh, good, because we've got to decide."

But when Oona opened the leather-trimmed trunk and Carol saw her clothes, she was caught off guard. Here was her friend, married to one of the richest and most celebrated artists of the century, and it was a piecemeal collection of odds and ends, really, nothing like the splendor she had been ready to swallow, along with whatever envy she thought might inevitably come up in her.

Oona smiled at her as they stood together at the standing trunk.

"I told you, darling. I really don't have much of a wardrobe."

"Oh, but these are all so exquisite," Carol lied.

"Darling, I saw your face fall when I opened the trunk"— Oona laughed—"so don't try that on me."

"Oh, but they are," Carol went on. Because it was one thing for Oona to make a joke of it, but *you* just didn't—ever. You just didn't.

And the two set about picking out what Oona would wear to the Academy Awards so Carol could make a complementary choice.

3

Driving home in her blue Rolls, Carol remembered an afternoon in Paris, in the fall of 1965, when she and Oona and Truman Capote had lunch together at the Méditerranée before a Balenciaga fashion show in the restaurant. Walter was making *Charade* and the Chaplins had come to town for a visit, and then Truman was in town, too. Suddenly, that afternoon in the restaurant, Oona had looked at her watch.

"Oh, my God," she said. "I've got to run. Charlie will be back at the hotel now."

Truman was upset by this.

"How can you live like that?" he asked her. "Don't you have any time for yourself?"

Carol immediately rose to her friend's defense.

"Truman, don't you realize that every woman in the world wants a man to need her like that?"

On the other hand, she thought as she drove by the Bel Air archway along Sunset, he had his point. They were always together, and apparently it was true, as Oona had told her but she'd never quite fathomed before now, she never really had the time to shop for herself but ran into a store while Charlie waited for her in the car and picked the first thing off the rack that she liked.

Well, but Oona had found a civilized man who adored her, who found her personal qualities—the look she had, the way she spoke, her very mind—delicious, like a kind of nectar, the answer to his own deepest dream of what a woman could be.

Walter had managed to find a copy of the screen test Oona

made for Charlie when they first met—they were planning to show it at the party tomorrow as a surprise for them both. And how beautiful she looked! The test ran for five minutes or so, silently, the camera holding on Oona's face as she responded to various directions to move to the right or the left. Her presence was luminous and full of her youthful sweetness, a graceful pliancy in response to her director's—to Charlie's—instructions.

She drove down into the intersection of Sunset and the Pacific Coast Highway, that odd little neighborhood in which the traffic waiting for the lights to change was almost as much a constant of the place as the tenants of the apartments that overlooked the scene. God knew who the people were in those run-down clapboard buildings across the highway from the beach. People struggling to get through each day, she supposed, the way she had struggled on Maroney Lane. Little nickel-and-dime lives, looking for the light.

The way she had looked, too, once upon a time. And found it, at long last, in Hollywood. Well, where else would it be? It was the last fairy tale out here. She knew it and so did everybody else. Everybody was just too guilty about it to admit it and take full pleasure in it.

She turned up onto Chautauqua, remembering an evening in New York when she and Bill and Oona and Charlie all had dinner together in the Champagne Room at El Morocco. Somehow the conversation that night came around to Rebecca West, whom Charlie and Bill both knew.

"Well," Bill said to Charlie, "I chased her around the living room one night in London, but nothing doing."

"Oh, really, old boy?" Charlie replied, "I'm surprised to hear it. Not with me. But let me assure you, you didn't miss a thing."

At that point, somebody gave Carol a violent kick under the table. She was barely able to keep from screaming in pain. Then quite off-handedly, Oona addressed her across the table.

"Darling," she said, "let's go to the powder room."

Not at all sure she would be able to walk, she nodded, got up, and tried the best she could to disguise her hobble as she moved through the restaurant with Oona.

In the powder room, Oona fixed her hair in the mirror and chatted casually about the evening. Carol was still in pain and very puzzled.

"Oona," she said finally, "just before we left the table, I don't know what happened. Somebody kicked me so hard I can barely walk."

"Oh, darling!" Oona turned from the mirror toward her. "I'm so sorry! I meant to kick *Charlie*. How dare he talk about that woman."

Well, that was a real *romance*—Oona and Charlie.

Carol parked her car in the garage and on her way through the kitchen she told Mary and Ray the garden party was on. Before she had left the bungalow, Oona had looked in on Charlie and come back to say that they should go ahead with it.

#

THAT NIGHT SHE DREAMED SHE WAS IN THE LITTLE PLANE over Paris that Daddy had taken her up in when she was nine or ten, the most marvelous, elegant little aircraft that he'd designed with Oliver Lucas, who designed the Rolls Royce. The plane was so little it was almost like flying oneself. And there was Paris below, and Daddy at the controls.

"This, darlin'," he said to her in the dream, "this is what love is."

"What do you mean, Daddy?" she asked, as they swung over the Eiffel Tower and the gray intricacies of the Paris streets below.

"Aviation," he answered with that quiet authority he had, as if he were speaking of the universally accepted solution of an equation that had been struggled with for centuries. She felt like a privileged witness in the realm of gods and goddesses.

Then she was wide awake, lying in bed in the master bedroom at the Palisades, and the digital clock said 3:09. Walter was asleep. Her husband, who looked out their window at night at the hills of Pacific Palisades, twinkling with the lights of homes, and said the view reminded him of the one from his old apartment on Central Park West—the apartment he'd taken so that they would have a place to be together.

Her two men, Daddy and Walter. Daddy at the Pink Turtle in the Beverly Wilshire, eating dinner with such elegant deliberation. Definitely not of the there's-no-tomorrow school she herself was a charter member of since her Hamburger Heaven days. And if his stories had the same careful, ruminative pace as his dining, even when the subject was as removed from her own immediate frame of reference as the laser fire extinguisher, for example, that he'd invented for the moon rocket—well, she would listen, or at least *appear* to be listening, every Sunday evening. Because this was the man who had taken her out of an ashcan.

Walter turned in his sleep and said "thank you" quite distinctly. His Academy Award acceptance speech? He was, after all, nominated for *Kotch* and, though not a front-runner (it would probably be Gene Hackman for *The French Connection*), he wasn't out of the running either.

"Thanks very much. Appreciate it." And walk off smiling, holding the Oscar.

She giggled in bed. 3:17.

"Go to sleep, sweetheart," Walter said from his side of the bed.

"I will, darling," she answered and touched his back, and

then took her hand away, and went on thinking in their pretty house. The perfect time to set everything in order. Every so often a car went by. Some L.A. mad people, roaming around with guns and dope and poison. Or was it just a neighbor coming home from a late party? The man who was the voice of all those cartoon characters, next door. A sweet man.

The last fairy tale—yes, that it was. Or if there ever *was* one, this was it. But then, it was complicated. Because Walter's heart attack had been the long, strange moment that suddenly brought it all to a head out here. His heart, her head? For in those few days—when his life had hung in the balance— she'd needed to think fast. *The Fortune Cookie* had only a few days of postproduction to go; he was in the clear as far as that went. But *The Odd Couple* had just been set up and if they'd had even a glimmer of how close to dying Walter was, they would have dropped him like that. No chance. (They'd never insure him.) It would be over.

She knew all that, somehow, as clearly as she'd ever known anything in life. An orphan, after all, is an orphan—no matter how you dress her, no matter what her address is, and no matter how much money she's got in the bank. You don't forget being hungry, and you don't forget having newspapers in your shoes because the soles have holes in them. Not as long as you live.

So what she did, during those two or three days, was to turn herself into a sort of moral pretzel, while she talked on the phone with the producer and the director and let them know that Walter was just fine—he had needed a rest; that was all it really amounted to—and was *so* looking forward to coming back to work. And these were people she knew and cared about, people whose own careers she might have been putting in jeopardy as she lied, but that was what it came to, and in the clinch you did what you had to do. If Walter died, it was over. But if Walter lived, and she'd blown it—it might be over too.

. . .

Each day she'd talk with him at his bedside in the hospital for a few minutes.

"Jesus," he said one afternoon, "I can't do plays again, after this. I'll never be sure I won't drop dead in the middle of a performance. I can't work the way I used to. I'm gonna end up back on the Lower East Side with no teeth."

"Darling," she answered, "I know you can't work on the stage again." In fact, she still wasn't sure he would ever be getting out of this bed. "But it's okay. Because you're going to be a very big movie star."

He looked at her, with the smile beginning in his eyes.

"You're crazy," he said. "Crazy."

And he closed his eyes again. He was right, of course. She was crazy. But somehow or other she also happened to be right. He made _The Odd Couple_ and became a movie star. The heart attack made a dent in his energy level that made it just right for the movies—whereas before he had been a little too "up," like Lee J. Cobb—and it seemed to happen overnight. And in a sense, it did. It just happened to be the darkest night of their lives.

3:42. So she had her fairy tale, too, like Oona. Beautiful Oona, knowing _exactly_ what the heart attack meant, the whole crazy business of a life after such a sudden, frightening showdown with mortality. The years somehow catching up at the very moment you thought things were going to be okay, at last. That dinner party at Mike Nichols's a few hours before on the night of Walter's heart attack—thank God they weren't there when it happened. Lillian Hellman had been there. And Walter sat next to Elizabeth Taylor, and joked about it later.

"I mean she's all right, but she's not _that_ great."

That was _three months_ later. After Oona had said to her, "Oh, darling, I know how you feel. Charlie hasn't had a heart attack but he's much older. And sometimes at night, lying in bed, I'll touch his foot with my foot and it's warm, and I'll think, 'He's alive. Right now, this moment, he's alive.'"

And that time she mailed Oona an unhappy letter, worrying over Walter's health, and right away she got back a thick envelope from her in Vevey. She put it aside until she got into bed that night, thinking she wouldn't have time until then to savor all her friend's thoughts and gossip and whatnot. But when she opened the envelope in her little rose-wallpapered room—where she slept when she didn't want to disturb Walter with her restlessness—all but one of the pages were blank, and something fell onto the bed, a clump of tissue paper with something in it. When she opened the paper, her eyeballs almost caved in. It was an old, exquisite diamond bracelet. Something priceless. But even more than that, something so *beautiful*.

On the sheet that wasn't blank, Oona had written: "Darling, I couldn't bear you sounding depressed, so I'm sending you this to cheer you up."

When she told Felicia Lemmon, her closest California friend, about it the next day, she still hadn't recovered from the shock of having the bracelet fall out onto the bed (sending it in the mail like that, my God, was even *dangerous*), and she was searching for some possible response to so extravagant, so out-of-this-world a present.

"I mean what do you say, Felicia? What *can* you say?" she asked over lunch at the Swiss Café on Rodeo.

But Felicia, with her dauntless savoir-faire, just shrugged.

"Send her a wire," she suggested. "'Still depressed. Keep 'em coming.'"

4:02. She would never sleep again. Wasn't it funny about Oona *never* showing the years? Although she supposed she did to the uninitiated eye, to someone removed from their lives, who didn't refer every look to the gallery of the years. You never really *saw* your closest friends because you looked beyond or into their faces, rather than at them, for the spark that kept your own life going.

Love was, then, after all, like aviation, as Daddy had pointed out to her over the elegant control panel in that little airplane over Paris in her dream. Like a Chagall. Except a Chagall was like flying oneself over a little town where the cow jumped over the moon. Because everybody knows everybody and being a stranger there is much harder than it is in a city. Being a stranger in a big family is even harder. Being an orphan is like not being able to find your mother in a big department store, even though you know she works as a millinery model there. It was like looking over and over again at the big clock up above the elevators but being too young to know how to read the time. And she was dreaming again.

5

IT WAS AFTER THE PARTY HAD ENDED, AFTER MIDNIGHT the following night, that Carol stood alone in her now darkened garden and remembered the pots of different-colored hyacinths all over the garden beside the red and white umbrella-shaded tables. A glorious, sunny Pacific Palisades day for Charlie and Oona—not too hot, the way it would be on the Beverly Hills flats. And you could see sailboats on the ocean from where they sat.

"Did you hire those boats for the party?" Charlie asked Walter early on, sitting with Oona in the dappled shade of their table. The party went off without a hitch. Cary Grant was there, and Danny Kaye; Oscar Levant, and Groucho.

"I walk much better than him, don't I?" Charlie whispered into Oona's ear about Groucho, Oona told her on the phone that evening.

Well, let New York condescend to Hollywood all they wanted, there was a magic to it they'd just be missing till the end of time. Carol had strolled here and there on their sunlit lawn, making sure this person had a drink and that person had some caviar, and everybody was happy and everything was perfect, while Charlie and Oona sat at the center of it all like two extraordinary flowers.

Lewis Milestone came, and Peter Bogdanovich, and Jean Renoir's widow, Dido. And there were some younger movie stars, sort of window dressing for the living legends. Martha Raye had phoned and asked to be invited, which of course they were delighted to do. She came in a big limousine and Charlie not only recognized her, he was delighted to see her—his eagerly amorous, but somehow unkillable nemesis in *Monsieur Verdoux*.

What was it Oona had told her about Jim Agee when *Monsieur Verdoux* came out and all the critics went after Charlie? They'd had a news conference in New York and they all baited Charlie about being a communist. Then Jim stood up at the back of the room and said, "Mr. Chaplin, I'm James Agee from *Time*. What do you think of a country that goes after an artist as you are being gone after?"

And Charlie couldn't quite hear him and asked him to repeat what he'd said, which he did, now somewhat embarrassed, and then Charlie just said "thank you" to Jim and called the press conference to an end. Agee—there was a hero: helping her get her feet on the other side of the Palisades, in that little house, so long ago now.

Oona and Charlie had left at around 3:30 and taken the limousine back to the hotel. Charlie was tiring. But the party went on and on—they managed a dinner for everybody around 8:00—and it wasn't over until it was nearly midnight.

Sudden quiet, now, on the dark lawn, and some crazy, jittery feeling after the party is over and the guests are gone and the world is the world again. She stood beside the big eucalyptus tree, her eyes, full of the years, glazing with tears.

6

SHE SLEPT LATE THE NEXT DAY. BY THE TIME SHE WOKE up, Walter had already left for the final Academy Awards rehearsal. He returned around four, took a quick nap, showered, dressed, and they took his red Mercedes (with WALTZ on the license plate) to the Dorothy Chandler Pavilion. She might have been shown on television for a moment as they went into the theater in the still-light evening. (Were Aram and Lucy watching? She knew Charlie, who was now nine, would be glued to their set in the den.) The fans cordoned off on both sides yelled "Hi, Walter!" and "I love you, Walter!" and he waved and blew a kiss to them before they went inside.

Then she and Oona were sitting beside each other between Walter, on the inside, and Charlie on the aisle—so he wouldn't have far to walk. The orchestra suddenly began the overture and Oona turned to her and whispered into her ear: "Do you realize where we *are?*"

That was Oona—who had stopped with Charlie at the Ritz that fall of 1965 when they'd all been in Paris, and Picasso and Cocteau had clambered through the hotel corridors to see Charlie; Oona—who had dined with royalty and prime ministers and statesmen on every continent. And now they were playing "Moon River" from the movie they'd made of Truman's *Breakfast at Tiffany's*—and both of their hearts were up in the sky.

In the end, after all, they were two of a kind: two students, not so much of their schools as of the movies, those very special movies of the thirties that taught you how to look, how to talk, how to kiss, and even, she supposed, in a funny way, how to think. She and Oona and Gloria, really any of the girls of their generation who were told that they were pretty, wanted to be in a white satin slinky dress in a penthouse with a cocktail shaker. Just like Veronica Lake.

It was on a warm spring afternoon, the first year after she and Oona had gotten out of school. They had gone to an address off Times Square that turned out to be a rather seedy office to see a producer about summer theater jobs. There were a number of other girls already in the waiting room, but progress was swift. When Carol's name was called by the secretary, she stood up, walked to the door she had seen the other girls go through, and entered the office. Here she found a man seated at a desk, and behind him a large, dirty window overlooking an air shaft. The man behind the desk was the stubby, leering cliché of a producer in a B movie, down to his cigar.

He had reviewed her résumé and photograph, and pointedly looked her up and down a few times. He didn't invite her to sit down on the beat-up dark wooden chair in the middle of the room, but told her about the coming summer stock season, including his plan to do a musical of some kind, maybe *Louisiana Purchase*.

Then he'd asked to see her legs. She wasn't sure at first what he had in mind, but he pointed his cigar and made a motion with it, indicating that she was to lift her skirt, a rather long one in the fashion of the early forties. She lifted it, tentatively, a few inches.

"More, doll, I want to see your legs."

She lifted the skirt up a little further.

"Come *on*," he said, exasperated. "I haven't got all day here."

"I'm sorry," she said, suddenly flushing. "I don't do that."

"You don't do that?" He looked at her.

She could have, at that moment, picked him up and thrown him out the window.

"That's right."

"Well, goodbye, doll," he said, dismissing her.

On her way out, she had turned back to him.

"Is there a ladies' room?"

"Door to your left."

She went into the bathroom and, with furious urgency, wrote with her red lipstick across the medicine-cabinet mirror: "Go fuck yourself!"

When she returned to the waiting room, she whispered to Oona to go to the loo before she went in to see the producer, so she'd have some idea what was in store.

Now here they were at the Academy Awards, sitting between two men who had scaled the heights of the art and industry of the movies. Seeing Charlie get what had so long been due him was marvelous and touching.

"You're all such sweet people," he said slowly, standing frail yet radiant before the standing ovation he received. These people, after all, were in large part professionals of the industry he'd had no small hand in creating.

7

"ARE YOU OKAY, PUSSYCAT?" WALTER SAID TO HER, AS they drove home that evening after the Awards.

"Oh yes, Poppy," she answered, sitting beside him as he drove along Sunset down into Mandeville Canyon. "I'm wonderful, darling. Why, did I do something terrible?"

"Oh, no," he said, smiling, "I just thought you might be sad because Oona and Charlie are leaving."

"Oh, I *am*," she answered, suddenly smelling honeysuckle on the air. Some little culvert they were passing, most likely. "That I *am*."

She sighed deeply, and inhaled the fragrance.

"Oh, darling, am I terribly, terribly old?" she asked.

"No, princess. You're younger than springtime."

"Good!" she said in her lower-pitched, comically curt voice, and breathed deeply of the dark, flower-laden air, and giggled.

C*O*DA

The two women laughed together, their laughter like a naughty but delightfully sung duet. Though they were not physically similar—Mrs. Matthau being blonder than Harlow and as lushly white as a gardenia, while the other had brandy eyes and a dark dimpled brilliance markedly present when [she] flashed smiles—one sensed they were two of a kind: charmingly incompetent adventuresses.

—Truman Capote, "La Côte Basque, 1965"

Up Above the World
1983

1

IT WAS LATE. AS SHE SOMETIMES LIKED TO DO, SHE'D GOT-
ten into her long embroidered red robe and slippers and picked
up after her little dinner party by herself, letting the help go for
the night. Now the evening's tipsiness had worn away into a
fine, thin edge of the mind and nerves. Everything had a luster.
The wind was out, buffeting the side of the Gracie Square penthouse, from time to time jolting, audibly, the living room's big
picture window with its long green drapes. The boys, of course,
were long gone to dreamland. Her assistant, Jean Dunn, long
asleep too, even with all the scheduling piled up this month when
she was in and out of the city each week—doing appearances
at department stores across the country to launch the new line
of bed linens with her own designs.

Her days, in fact, were as brightly and intricately plotted for
her now as one of her own design originals. But with Wyatt's
death, the nights could be suddenly huge and only approxi-
mately charted. But then of course she was supposed to be asleep.
But the fact was she wasn't asleep. She was wide, even wildly,
awake, and alone, and up above the whole world. Here in her
much celebrated living room, filled with the photographs and
paintings and fabrics that spoke to her of virtually all the epochs
of her life, like a kind of pleasure palace of her own past—and
what had it all amounted to? Starting, say, with her memory of
her father, Reggie, in the next room dying of acute alcoholism?
That *earliest* memory—indeed, one she hadn't even known she

had, until, in the late sixties, she had taken LSD under a doctor's supervision and regressed to relive that primal scene of her infancy. Suddenly there she was in her nursery, fully aware that her father was dying in the next room. So frustrated she was at her helplessness! Her own powerful will and consciousness ridiculously imprisoned in the body of an infant, her own condition, in fact, a kind of ironic reverse image of her father's. Poor Reggie, only forty-four—but bereft, it seemed from the beginning, of any will at all.

Well, something had taken care of that element in *her;* added to that, the years had made her a pro. Oh, she certainly knew she was that—and that it was no little achievement, either. She had long since observed how surprisingly few of them there were around. But she was also a woman, and no longer a young one, and, at this hour of the night, unless she made stricter arrangements than she'd managed tonight, all too likely to be at loose ends.

She sat down on her rose-print sofa beneath the picture window and gazed across the room at the American Impressionist beach scene near the room's entrance. She'd found it at the Berry-Hill Gallery at the same time she'd purchased the Sargent portrait of her mother, life-size and full-length, now in the dining room. She'd finally gotten her mother to herself—not to mention as close to the kitchen as she'd probably ever been. Well, that would have to be as close as you could come, anyway, in the most beautiful black gown anyone had ever worn. Poor Mommy, younger than she herself was now, overlooking (though turned to three-quarter profile) her daughter's dinner parties.

She picked up the telephone beside the book of Van Vechten's portraits on the glass-topped coffee table and dialed Carol's number in the Palisades. Carol had moved back into the house a few months before after two years of remodeling. Every room now had a rose pattern on the walls. She was smiling to herself before she was halfway through the digits. It wouldn't be midnight yet in California, and Carol's moon came out just around now—unless, of course, she was sound asleep with Walter, and she was going to be in big trouble for waking them both up.

Two rings.

"Hello." Carol always sounded as if she'd either just woken up, or just sprinted to exhaustion to the receiver.

"Darling!"

"Oh, Gloria! I'm so glad you called. I'm sitting up in my beautiful room, and I'm going crazy because I've got no one to talk to, and I'm so excited!"

Gloria was laughing. It was like finding a sort of fun house mirror-image of herself all the way across the continent.

She had seen the house a month before when she'd been in Los Angeles for two days. Carol had awaited her verdict with that air of excited anticipation that as a painter she recognized from the nights of her openings. And the house *was* marvelous—and she'd said so virtually the minute she was inside the front door. Now she said it again.

"Darling, the house is *so* beautiful!"

"Is it? *Really?* You know I've driven everyone absolutely crazy, and Walter is never going to speak to me again when he sees the full bill. I've been trying to feed it to him in installments, but he gets this look in his eye sometimes and I have a feeling he knows..."

"Oh, sweetheart, it's the most beautiful house of all!"

"But, darling," Carol said, having apparently settled to her satisfaction this first order of business, and vocally switching gears, "I'm glad you called for another reason. I'll tell you why. I'm worried about Oona."

"Oh, Oona... My God, she's just so—*difficult*. I mean I've tried, you know. I've called; I've written; I've sent flowers. But *really*..."

"She misses him."

"Oh, I know. I know. But please. I mean I miss Wyatt, too, you know. Of course I do."

2

It had been Wyatt who told her to use her name. After all these years, the struggle of trying to deal with the robber baron legacy that seemed so foreign to her own deepest instincts, he had simply said, Why not? Let it work for you—Gloria Vanderbilt. Just use it. Let them put your name, let them even use that beautiful, iconographic signature you have, on a pair of jeans—as Murjani had in fact proposed. And that had been the turning point. After years of her own indecisiveness—a few shows of her paintings, a few acting jobs—and the public idea of her as a poor little rich girl, he'd let her go to her own possibility—and he'd been absolutely right. And, damn it, she did miss him. The heart attack had just been—so sudden. Overnight, he was gone. Just gone. And that it had come within a week after Charlie had died was some kind of awful irony—all those years waiting for the moment they all knew would come with Charlie and Oona, and never for a moment suspecting it would be coming a few days later in her own life, with a husband thirty years younger than Charlie. She had assumed, of course, that Carol would already be with Oona, but instead she had come at once from California to be with Gloria in New York.

"I *know* you miss him, darling. Of course you do. I told you how moving it was to see you and Carter and Anderson together when I came."

"Oh, but it meant *so much* for you to come then."

"Well, darling, of course I came. I mean I knew Oona would have the whole family around her. I knew that. No, of course I wanted to be with you there. Seeing the three of you sitting together on the living room sofa those afternoons, the boys doing their homework, and all of you so watchful of one another, so caring, from moment to moment—now _that's_ a family. I know you had that with Stan and Chris, but Wyatt gave that to you again. And it's still there even though he's gone, because Carter and Anderson are with you."

"Oh, they really got me through it. That's for sure."

"Anyway...." Carol sighed, switching gears again. "You know—it's funny with Oona. Don't think badly of her."

Gloria shifted on the couch, put her head against a corner pillow and, after letting her slippers fall, drew her feet up. In one corner of the window now, she saw the colored lights of an airplane silently moving toward the darkness.

"Darling," she answered Carol, "I love her. I _love_ her. But I just don't know what to do. I mean whenever we talk it's 'oh yes' and 'oh darling' and 'of course'—but what does it all mean? I mean I don't know what's happening with her."

"She just misses him. You know I went to Switzerland. Well, Walter and I were in Venice for the Ingrid Bergman tribute and she sent _two_ cars—one for us, and one for our bags, do you believe that?—and they drove us to Vevey. And when we got to the house, she was there at the door to meet us. And you know how I've been flying to see her and be with her these last few years since Charlie died—I mean whenever I thought maybe it might do some good?"

"Of course."

"Well, Walter's always gone along with it, which is unusual for him, really, but he adores Oona, too. When she came out here for the first time after Charlie died, did I tell you what he said—when he saw her walking on the beach at Trancas, for the first time without Charlie? Did I tell you this?"

"No, I don't think so." The plane had traversed the window and vanished into farther parts of the sky.

"He said, 'She looks like someone with half her body gone.'"

"Now you're going to make me cry."

"Yes, but listen: when we arrived at Vevey after all my trips to her, all these little first-aid missions, you know—I mean I'm not going to tell you they weren't all wonderful, relaxing vacations for *me*, because they were, but anyway—she comes out of the front door looking absolutely radiantly healthy and beautiful. She can still do that. And Walter just looked at me and said, 'Who's the guy?'"

"'Who's the guy?'"

"In other words, I'd have to be having an affair every time I told him I had to go see her, because obviously she's in wonderful shape."

"Oh—of course."

3

"BUT SEE, SHE'S FUNNY THAT WAY," CAROL WENT ON, as Gloria relaxed more deeply now into the contours of her sofa, "because we had a beautiful dinner, and the whole evening was just lovely. She gets along with Walter, and so it was all just very, very nice. Although, of course, I was feeling a little odd because of what Walter said. I mean he really *would* have to wonder about everything because she was absolutely fine. Perfect. Wonderful."

"Well, but..." There was the deep honk of a barge now, twelve floors below and whatever distance away, on the East River. Gloria looked out at the quietness of the living room— the chair upholstered in green English chintz beside the coffee table. Did things go to sleep in a room at night when people went to bed? Or was that when the party began, like in that old Saturday matinee cartoon?

"Well, this is the thing, though. The next day she didn't come down from her room."

"You're kidding?"

"Nope. Breakfast, lunch, and dinner. Nothing. I mean her staff works beautifully, you know. We were very well taken care of. But she wasn't there."

"That's terrible!"

"And, of course, we were going the next morning. So I decided I'd go up and see her. Just to say goodbye. Or whatever."

"Well, you just should have told her off! I mean either she gets out of that bed . . ."

"Oh, no. You can't do that with Oona. You just can't. In the first place, it wouldn't do a bit of good. Really."

Here Gloria was, in the middle of the night, suddenly feeling a surge of anger at Oona. Or could it be that it was actually at something—or some*one*—else? Could she really be this angry at Oona, that dear, shy woman who had been her friend so long? It didn't make sense. But what was it then? At Wyatt, maybe? For dying? Carol somehow understood so much more than she did. And yet, didn't Oona *absolutely need* someone to get her up and out and back into the world? Work had been her own salvation after Wyatt's death. That she knew.

"Anyway," Carol went on, "I went up and knocked on her door and she said, 'Who is it?' and I said, 'It's me, it's Carol,' and she said, 'Oh, come in, darling.' So I opened the door and went in. The shades were down so it was dark, although it was still really afternoon outside. And I just sat down in a chair near the end of the bed. I mean Oona and I have worn each other's dresses and I don't have to pretend with her. That's really the great pleasure of knowing her, darling. You don't have to pretend with Oona—about *anything*. So I sat down in a chair and we didn't even talk."

"In the dark?"

"That's right. But then—well, after a few minutes of just this quietness, you know—she just said, she said, 'It's nice in here, isn't it?'"

"Oh boy."

"Just 'It's nice in here, isn't it?' So I thought about that for a moment, you know, because here we were in the dark, two old bags in a dark room, and she says it's nice. I mean what does it mean?"

Gloria started laughing. "Darling, I love you. You're sane. No, you really are."

"Put that in a letter to Walter right away. He's got to hear that right now."

"Not coming from me, though."

"Oh, sweetheart, he loves you. He's forgotten about any old fight you might have had. He really doesn't hold on to things like that and he never has. That's one thing I've learned from him."

"Well, I just think *he's* marvelous."

"Well, he thinks you're marvelous."

"But go on..."

"Sweetheart, will you hold for just one second," Carol said with unusual urgency.

"Sure," she answered, and held the phone while her friend went away.

4

A HELICOPTER WAS MAKING ITS WAY SOMEWHERE OUT OF view—that loud, slicing noise, as if it were cutting the darkness up into black party streamers. For her midnight party with Carol? She gazed across the night-glazed stillness of her living room at the American Impressionist beach scene again—the sun sparkling on the waves somewhere. Maybe the Hamptons, in the early 1900s. Carol was back.

"Sorry, darling. I *had* to go get another of Mary's baked apples."

"Oh, that's all right. Sounds delicious."

"Anyway, let me finish this. She says, 'It's nice in here, isn't it?' and I sort of sit with that for a moment. I mean, you know, *everything*, in a certain light, is true, just as, in another light, it's also false. That's what Einstein was saying, I think. And that's the great beauty of life, and also the great terror."

"Everything? What about the years, darling? They're too true to be false."

"Well, that's true. But what about when you're in love and forget about time and think you're beautiful and young again? That's what still happens to me with Walter. Well, you know I'm convinced being in love is partly loving the way someone sees *you*."

"Oh, of course!"

"You know, that's at least *part* of it. So anyway, I'm sitting with Oona and I sort of see what she's saying, I guess, or think I do, and I say to her, 'Well, yes, I can see how you would feel that way'—about the room being nice, you know—'It's cool. And it's dark. And it's quiet.' And then, rather softly, she just said, 'Like where Charlie is.'"

"Like where Charlie is—?"

"That's right. Like where Charlie is."

There were tears in Gloria's eyes now, and she sat up, angry and moved at the same time. Her poor, infuriating friend, who wouldn't move when the train came hurtling down the tracks, who had no work to keep her to the daily round. Who let herself wander, as if she could trust herself to the night on the other side of this picture window.

"Well," Carol continued, "that sort of threw me for a moment, you know."

"Oh, she's just *impossible*. I know her—in my own reactions, you know—but thank God I've got work to do each morning."

"Well, it was funny because there I was in that room with her, and I was suddenly thinking of you."

"Me? Really? *Why?*"

"Isn't that funny? Let me tell you why. Oona and I are very

great friends, really, you know, deep friends. And darling, you know how much I love you. And how much you mean to me. So I don't mean to compare our friendship. When you love someone the way I love both of you there are no comparisons. But it's different—what I share with you, and what I share with Oona. Sometimes I think Oona and I are *too* close. We've stepped through each other and come out on the other side. And when we're together it's almost like we're alone, but together, do you know what I mean?"

"I think that's marvelous—that you have that."

"Well, it is and it isn't. Because, you know, in a funny way people really *are* what they pretend to be. I mean aspiration is *everything*, darling. And really you're the one who's taught me that more than anyone else in the world. And that's why I thought of you. And I said to her then, I said, 'Oh, yes, Oona. *I* love it here. You know me. But darling, you need a real person for a friend. Not an old stick-in-the-mud like me. You need someone to roust you out of here right away! You need—Gloria!' And we both laughed about that—because, you know, it really *was* you that we needed just at that moment."

5

THE NIGHT STRETCHED BEFORE HER LIKE A LUXURIOUS black velvet carpet, with Carol's voice on the other end—a three-thousand-mile-long carpet with the stars you never saw in Manhattan somehow up there in the sky twinkling like diamonds over their lives, the long fabric of understanding their friendship had given them. It was an idea for a collage, maybe? Friendship—those moments it made in one's history that were larger than the story they were part of. Suddenly there was the moment when the heart was full—of love, of tears, of both—and it was then that time really came to a stop and you saw everything with the eyes of love, which was something like eternity. What was it in Carol that had always triggered at least the possibility of this seeing, that seemed to release Gloria from the rigidities of her ordinary, time-bound self? It was hard to say, and yet, at times over the years she'd caught some flicker of a memory playing through her friend's daffy style—her look and her talk—yet even now she scarcely dared to make the connection, although it had grown more and more familiar over the years.

Could it be that Carol possessed something of her mother's, Big Gloria's, childlike charm and beauty and innocence? Was this what had made her so strangely protective in her feeling for her? Well, she knew her mother had never possessed Carol's wit, that original personal style she had always had. No, but there was an even more essential quality—like a child looking wide-eyed at the candles on a birthday cake, knowing the presents were to come—that sense of the *adventure*, that anticipation of life's rewards, the sweet innocence of such expectations. Of course, her mother's disillusionment, in the end, had by degrees transformed the poor woman's youth and beauty into a querulous fragility, like some exotic blossom of the hothouse that had shriveled all too swiftly in the light of ordinary day. But somehow Carol, with all her innate sweetness, was a hardier breed. Was this why Gloria had been somehow moved even when her friend had been angry with her? Yes, even then, when she herself was feeling the sting of Carol's anger, she had been, in a deeper part of herself, cheering her on for her courage.

For by then, of course, she knew that she herself wasn't made of such softness as Big Gloria, and yet to sense its essence again in her friend, yet this time given a fighting chance because Carol was *more* than simple, feminine sweetness, made her—well, it filled her heart. And that was important—oh, but how important that had been! As she grew strong through the years, and now, most of all, when she had a public presence in her strength, it was her friend alone who could—as if by magic—open those doors in her: doors to the rooms of her own deeper life that gave the resonance to her work, that kept the colors alive in her. It was the strength of what she did: that she could open the rooms of her lost, crazy-quilt of a childhood with her mother and Thelma, and discover—well, say, the South of France.

She tried to shake her reverie now: it could wait. She wanted to tell Carol a story. "Darling, you won't believe what happened in New Orleans last week?"

"What?" Carol answered, drinking something now. Probably one of her ubiquitous Coca-Colas.

"Well, I did an afternoon at Macy's, meeting shoppers, and everyone was *so* terribly sweet. They really come out, you know, I mean just lines and lines of people, and all of them so darling."

"Oh, but you deserve it...."

"Well, anyway, in the line, I couldn't help noticing these three really extraordinarily beautiful—I mean really *knock-out*—black girls, you know, as they moved closer and closer."

"Ah-hanh."

"And, well, then, there they were, I mean in front of me. And I mean just so elegant..."

"Aren't they, really, the *most* beautiful, don't you think?"

"Well," Gloria said, laughing a little breathlessly, "this is what I was thinking, and then, I don't know what it was, but suddenly I knew..."

"What?"

"They were..."

"Men!" Carol suddenly finished for her, in a voice pitched low with comic betrayal.

"That's right!" Gloria answered. "But, darling, you wouldn't *believe* how gorgeous..."

"Those *cunts!*" Carol pronounced, laughing.

"'We want to be just like you,' they said to me," Gloria told her, laughing too.

6

"I WAS REALLY SORT OF UNCONSCIOUS THEN, YOU KNOW," Carol remarked some time later, more or less in passing, after the two had settled briefly on what they referred to in their private shorthand as the "Mrs. Irvine" story.

It had taken place in New York before Carol married Bill, but after Gloria married Pat di Cicco. Carol had come to their apartment on East 57th Street, and asked for Gloria's help. She thought she might be pregnant by Bill, but wasn't certain. Nobody else must know. But, of course, Carol herself needed to know immediately.

Gloria decided to take her to her own personal physician, but they would need to disguise her so the doctor wouldn't recognize her as a famous New York debutante, unmarried, lest word of the pregnancy sneak out to the gossip columnists.

The day of the appointment, the two spent the whole morning getting Carol dressed. It was a little like playing dolls with a grown-up-sized doll. They gave Carol a turban to hide her blond hair, perhaps a giveaway. And of course a turban wouldn't need to be undone for a gynecological examination. They gave her a pair of giant sunglasses.

"I looked like I'd just landed from Mars," Carol quipped. "We can admit it now."

"Oh, you were *so* glamorous," Gloria answered.

"Only if you like flying saucers—that's what I looked like."

"Stop!"

Gloria had also given Carol a name, Mrs. Irvine, when she made the appointment for her with her doctor, telling him only that she was a close personal friend. The examination went off without a hitch; and the good news followed that Carol wasn't pregnant.

Then, six months later, Gloria went for her own regular checkup with the doctor. By this time, Carol and Bill had gotten married. It was as she was leaving his office that afternoon that her doctor called to Gloria as an afterthought, "Oh, and say hello to Mrs. Saroyan for me."

How had he known? How had he penetrated their most intrepid contrivances? It was Gloria's first inkling that Carol, like her, lived her life in a sort of social goldfish bowl.

"No, I was really unconscious during those years," Carol continued, "which is why I think I'm so involved with all the spy literature now."

"But why *is* that?" Gloria knew her friend was steeped in the lore of Kim Philby and all the others, and even had MI6—the initials of the British secret service—on the vanity license plate of her Rolls.

"Because," Carol answered, "I really want to *know* what was going on during those years when all I did was live and breathe Bill Saroyan morning, noon, and night. Those were such important years I missed."

"You were too good for him." It was somehow easier to talk about him now, two years after his death.

"Oh, sweetheart, that's all done now, and really, you know, with Bill gone now, I don't think I even hate him any more. I mean I realize he tried his best, he just really *was* impossible; and I didn't know it, and I don't think *he* did, either. But the point is—we were a *war* generation, darling. I remember looking out the window at 420 Park and watching the Seventh Regiment march down Park Avenue one afternoon. All those boys who were literally, you know, New York's finest: Kingdon Gould, and Stevie Hopkins—who was killed in the Pacific—and Eric Seiber, who was this blond god at Princeton, and then came back from the war in a wheelchair. And Geoff, of course, too."

"Oh, yes, Geoff."

"You know sometimes I wonder why you didn't marry *him*."

"Geoff Jones?" Gloria was smiling to herself.

"Well," Carol went on, "I could tell at the Southampton party that he was still just as mad about you now as he was at Princeton." Six months after Charlie's and Wyatt's deaths, in the spring of 1979, Gloria had given a party for Carol and Oona and herself at her Southampton house, a sort of birthday party for the decades of their friendship.

"Oh, darling, that's crazy. I was Geoff's *caddy* when he was at Princeton. He had me running all over the golf course one afternoon after his golf balls."

"Really?"

"Yes, and he thought it was so *funny*. I decided then and there I'd never marry him."

"But you never said anything about it to him?"

"Oh, no. No, I didn't tell him."

"You're such a great lady."

"Oh, please. But I do love Geoff very much as a friend."

7

IT WAS *SO* LATE. SHE'D REALLY DONE IT THIS TIME. SHE'D be running on empty tomorrow—today, that is. But Carol was so fascinating, and so much fun, and the time flew, and she knew too that her heart, under the tight wraps of her jet-powered month of department store appearances, was out tonight, flying like a crazy kite in the transcontinental night. Carol had just described an experience she'd had, at the edge of sleep, of leaving her body and having her consciousness rise up into the night.

"The universe is *black*. That's what I discovered."

"Black?"

"That's right, like the night, but with millions and millions of stars."

"Oh, it sounds beautiful."

Her collage again. Or a design, maybe. But for what? A perfume box?

"Darling, you're tired," Carol told her suddenly.

"Oh, sweetheart, I'm having so much fun. But, you know, I'm supposed to be up in about a half an hour."

"Oh my God. We'll talk soon again. Really we will. We *should*, you know."

"Oh yes, we should," Gloria affirmed. "It does my heart good."

"And mine."

"And you tell that Oona that I want her up in the morning from now on—by nine at the latest!"

"You should tell her that yourself," Carol said. "It's just what she needs."

"No, I can't. I love her, but she's got to do it herself. I know she'll survive. I did, and she will too."

"Oh, of course she will. Well, I told you how beautiful she looked. She can still do that."

"I'm glad. Well—goodnight, darling. I love you," Gloria said.

"Goodnight, darling. I love *you*," Carol answered.

After she put down the receiver, Gloria raised and turned her head to look through her window down at the East River, brownish-pink now in the dawn. There was a barge out on the water, three tiny figures on the deck. She put her slippers on and got up and walked through the apartment to her bedroom to shower and dress. The business of the day had begun.